# NECRONS

### THEIR NUMBER IS LEGION,
### THEIR NAME IS DEATH

# CONTENTS

## PRODUCED BY GAMES WORKSHOP IN NOTTINGHAM

With thanks to the Mournival for their additional playtesting services

Games Workshop Ltd, Willow Rd, Lenton, Nottingham, NG7 2WS
games-workshop.com

# INTRODUCTION

**You hold in your hands the definitive guide to the Necrons, a race of deathless androids from the prehistory of the universe. Under your command, they will rise from the sands of time to wage war upon the younger races. This book will help you assemble your collection of Necrons Citadel Miniatures into a powerful army, bound together by military structure and dynastic heraldry.**

Beneath the skin of the galaxy lurks the eldritch menace known as the Necrons. Having long ago made a devil's bargain to swap the frailties of flesh for undying metal, they now stir to murderous wakefulness on worlds uncounted after millions of years of slumber, and seek to reclaim the stars from those who have usurped them.

Though they have the nigh-indestructible bodies of killer machines, the Necrons possess a macabre and captivating character, and their armies are many and varied. In collecting and gaming terms, this permits you freedom to build whatever force you like, from whichever models appeal to you the most. Whether it be a council of haughty Overlords and genius Crypteks fighting to outdo one another, a relentless phalanx of android warriors, a fast-moving swarm of Canoptek constructs, or an entire dynasty ready for war, no other army can match the resilience and sophisticated weaponry of the Necrons on the battlefield.

Building and painting Necrons is a unique and exciting challenge for collectors of any ability. The leaders of the Necron forces are imposing and often eccentric figures, each bearing distinctive weapons and artefacts of great power. Necron Warriors look truly stunning when arranged in rank and file, their metal bodies reflecting the lurid energy signatures of their gauss weaponry. The war machines that bolster them dwarf those of the galaxy's lesser races, and have the power to match. All can be painted in the colour scheme of your chosen dynasty, with icons, scripts and as great a level of detail as you choose to apply.

On the pages that follow you will find all the information you need to collect a Necrons army and field it upon the tabletop in the full and magnificent splendour of days long past.

THE NECRON LEGIONS: This section introduces the Necrons in all their resurgent glory, details the tragic twist of fate that condemned them to an eternity as soulless androids, and offers an account of their campaigns of reclamation since their awakening.

THE IMMORTAL ARMIES: Here you will find an inspirational showcase of beautifully painted Necrons miniatures, complete with dynastic colour schemes and example armies.

THE DYNASTIES ASCENDANT: This section includes datasheets, wargear lists and weapon rules for every Necrons unit for you to use in your games of Warhammer 40,000.

CODE OF WAR: Finally, this section provides additional rules, matched play points and a selection of Stratagems and Relics to transform your collection of miniatures into an implacable Necron army ready to take back the stars.

*To play games with your army, you will need a copy of the Warhammer 40,000 rules. To find out more about Warhammer 40,000 or download the free core rules, visit warhammer40000.com.*

Deathless. Relentless. Incapable of doubt. The Necrons march, intent upon reconquering a galaxy that was once shackled to their will. Aeons of long sleep have broken down the dynasties, eroding them to the point of madness and beyond, but still they are death incarnate. woe to those who resist their claims to dominion, for they will be reduced to atoms and scattered upon the wind.

# THE NECRON LEGIONS

**Like a whispered breath that grows into a raging storm, the Necrons are returning. Beneath the surface of countless worlds, soulless armies stir. Inhuman Overlords raise their gaze to the stars, their minds turning once more to dreams of domination and war.**

For sixty million years the Necrons have slumbered, their tomb worlds filled with dormant armies and inactive war machines. Now they are awakening as if from half-remembered nightmares, and the galaxy shudders at their return. From vast crypt-fortresses, burnished legions emerge into the dying light of the 41st Millennium, a steel sea rippling beneath the crackling energy discharge of esoteric battle engines. Swarming metal Scarabs, talon-limbed horrors and spectral assassins accompany them, their alien minds focused on a single purpose – to reclaim the stars.

However, time has wounded the Necrons in ways their ancient enemies could not. What was once a galaxy-spanning network of dynasties under the watchful gaze of the Silent King is now a scattering of isolated domains. Entire tomb worlds have been lost, their star systems consumed by celestial catastrophe or plundered by younger races. Others have suffered technological failure, the cold hands of entropy destroying vital systems and dooming their inhabitants to an endless sleep. Even amongst those who have woken, the scars of time can be seen. This is no more evident than in the minds of the Overlords, who are often touched by madness. Their personalities warped and distorted by millennia of stasis, they pursue their own damaged agendas to the woe of all they encounter. Yet, despite those lost to the ravages of time, a great many remain. These vast alien armies stand ready for war, determined to return the Necrons to their rightful place among the stars.

On countless planets, legions of metallic warriors march forth from ancient vaults and into the cold radiance of fading suns. Those of other races with the misfortune to have made their homes upon these worlds are annihilated in storms of gauss fire and particle beams, for even the Necrons' most basic weaponry can strip a body to its constituent atoms in seconds.

The fires of battle glint from dense metal alloy and iron cabling, for the Necrons are not mere creatures of flesh and blood. Bullets ricochet from their impervious hides, las-blasts leave scorch marks but cause no lasting damage. Even those Necrons blasted to pieces by heavy weaponry slowly piece themselves back together, their reanimation protocols seeing decapitated heads reattach to necks and disembodied limbs crawl across the ravaged soil to reunite with their torsos. It is a shocking sight, to witness those thought slain stand up and take bloody revenge on their would-be killers. Such cold and unremitting destruction is the fate of all who oppose the Necrons' advance. In the eyes of the phaerons and Overlords, the young races are simply the dust that has gathered between the cracks of their empire – and, like dust, they must be swept away.

*'Witness that which the lesser races have achieved in our absence. How pitiful their accomplishments, and how crude their strategies. They fool themselves into believing that they march towards their own grand destiny, when the truth is far simpler – their civilisations are mere footnotes in the glorious history of the Necrontyr.'*

*- Imotekh the Stormlord*

# IN THE BEGINNING

The race that would become the Necrons began their existence under a fearsome, scourging star, billions of years before Mankind evolved on Terra. Assailed at every moment by solar winds and radiation storms, the flesh-and-blood Necrontyr became a morbid people whose precarious lifespans were riven by constant loss. Their dynasties were founded on the anticipation of demise, and the living were thought of as no more than temporary residents hurrying through the sepulchres and tombs of their ancestors.

Unable to find peace on their own planet, the Necrontyr blindly groped out towards other worlds. Using stasis-crypts aboard slow burning torch-ships, they began to colonise other planets. Little by little, the Necrontyr dynasties spread ever further, until much of the galaxy answered to their rule.

As time wore on, further strife came to the Necrontyr. While their territory grew ever wider and more diverse, the unity that had made them strong was eroded, and bitter wars were waged as entire realms fought to win independence. Eventually, the Triarch – the ruling council of the Necrontyr – realised that the only hope of unity lay in conflict with an external enemy, but there were few who could prove a credible threat. Only the Old Ones, first of all the galaxy's sentient life forms, were a prospective foe great enough to bind the Necrontyr to a common cause. Such a war was simplicity itself to justify, for the Necrontyr had ever rankled at the Old Ones' refusal to share the secrets of eternal life. So did the Triarch declare war upon the Old Ones. At the same time, they offered amnesty to any secessionist dynasties who willingly returned to the fold. Thus lured by the spoils of victory and the promise of immortality, the separatist realms abandoned rebellion and the War in Heaven began.

## THE WAR IN HEAVEN

The terrible campaigns that followed could fill a library in their own right, but the underlying truth was a simple one: the Necrontyr could never win. Their superior numbers and technologies were constantly outmanoeuvred by the Old Ones' mastery of the webway portals. In but a span of centuries, the Necrontyr were pushed back until they were little more than an irritation, a quiescent peril clinging to isolated and forgotten worlds. In the face of defeat, the unity of the Necrontyr began to fracture once more. No longer did the prospect of a common enemy have any hold over the disparate dynasties. Scores of generations had now lived and died in the service of an unwinnable war, and many Necrontyr dynasties would have gladly sued for peace had the ruling Triarch permitted it.

Thus began the second iteration of the Wars of Secession, more widespread and ruinous than any that had come before. So fractured had the Necrontyr dynasties become by then that, had the Old Ones been so inclined, they could have wiped them out with ease. Faced with the total collapse of their rule, the Triarch searched desperately for a means of restoring order. In this, their prayers were answered, though the price would be incalculably high.

## THE COMING OF THE COSMIC ONES

It was during the reign of Szarekh that the godlike beings known as the C'tan first blighted the Necrontyr. It is impossible to say for certain how the Necrontyr first came to encounter the C'tan, though many misleading, contradictory and one-sided accounts of these events exist. The dusty archives of Solemnace claim it was but an accident, a chance discovery made by a stellar probe during the investigation of a dying star. The Book of Mournful Night, held under close guard in the Black

Library's innermost sanctum, tells rather that the raw hatred that the Necrontyr held for the Old Ones sang out across space, acting as a beacon the C'tan could not ignore. Howsoever contact occurred, the shadow of the C'tan fell over the oldest dynasties first. Some Necrontyr actively sought the C'tan's favour and oversaw the forging of living metal bodies to contain the star gods' nebulous essence. Thus clad, the C'tan took the shapes of the Necrontyr's half-forgotten gods, hiding their own desires beneath cloaks of obsequious subservience.

So it was that one of the C'tan came before the Silent King, acting as forerunner to the arrival of his brothers. Amongst its own kind, this C'tan was known as the Deceiver, for it was wilfully treacherous. Yet the Silent King knew not the C'tan's true nature, and instead granted the creature an audience. The Deceiver spoke of a war, fought long before the birth of the Necrontyr, between the C'tan and the Old Ones. It was a war, he said, that the C'tan had lost. In the aftermath, and fearing the vengeance of the Old Ones, he and his brothers had hidden themselves away, hoping one day to find allies with whom they could finally bring the Old Ones to account. In return for aid, the Deceiver assured, he and his brothers would deliver everything that the Necrontyr craved. Unity could be theirs once again, and the immortality that they had sought for so long would finally be within their grasp. No price would there be for these great gifts, the Deceiver insisted, for they were but boons to be bestowed upon valued allies.

Thus did the Deceiver speak, and who can say how much of his tale was truth? It is

---

### THE TRIARCH AND THE SILENT KING

From the earliest days, the rulers of individual Necrontyr dynasties were themselves governed by the Triarch, a council of three phaerons. The head of the Triarch was known as the Silent King, for he addressed his subjects only through the other two phaerons who ruled alongside him. Nominally a hereditary position, the uncertain lifespans of the Necrontyr ensured that the title of Silent King nonetheless passed from one royal dynasty to another many times. The final days of the Necrontyr occurred in the reign of Szarekh, last of the Silent Kings.

doubtful whether even the Deceiver knew, for trickery had become so much a part of his existence that he could no longer divine its root. Yet his words held sway over Szarekh who, like his ancestors before him, despaired of the divisions that were tearing his people apart. For long months he debated the matter with the Triarch and the nobles of his Royal Court. Through it all, the only dissenting voice was that of Orikan, the court astrologer, who foretold that the alliance would bring about a renaissance of glory, but destroy forever the soul of the Necrontyr people. Yet desire and ambition swiftly overrode caution, and Orikan's prophecy was dismissed. A year after the Deceiver had presented his proposition, the Triarch agreed to the alliance, and so forever doomed their race.

## BIOTRANSFERENCE

With the pact between Necrontyr and C'tan sealed, the star gods revealed the form that immortality would take, and the great biotransference began. Colossal bio-furnaces roared day and night, consuming bodies of weak flesh and replacing them with enduring forms of living metal. As the cyclopean machines clamoured, the C'tan swarmed about the biotransference sites, drinking in the torrent of cast-off life energy and growing ever stronger.

As Szarekh watched the C'tan feast on the life essence of his people, he realised the terrible depth of his mistake. In many ways, he felt better than he had in decades, the countless aches and uncertainties of organic life now behind him. His new machine body was far mightier than the frail form he had tolerated for so long, and his thoughts were swifter and clearer than they had ever been. Yet there was an emptiness gnawing at his mind, an inexpressible hollowness of spirit that defied rational explanation. In that moment, he knew with cold certainty that the price of physical immortality had been the loss of his soul. With great sorrow the Silent King beheld the fate he had brought upon his people: the Necrontyr were now but a memory, the soulless Necrons born in their place.

Though the price had been incalculably steep, biotransference had fulfilled all of the promises that the C'tan had made. Even the lowliest of Necrontyr was blessed with immortality – age and radiation could little erode their new bodies, and only the most terrible of injuries could destroy them utterly. Likewise, the Necrons enjoyed a

unity that the Necrontyr had never known, though it was achieved through tyranny rather than consent. The biotransference process had embedded command protocols in every mind, granting Szarekh the unswerving loyalty of his subjects. At first, the Silent King embraced this unanimity, for it was a welcome reprieve from the chaos of recent years. However, as time wore on he grew weary of his burden but dared not sever the command protocols, lest his subjects turn on him seeking vengeance for the terrible curse he had visited upon them.

## VICTORY AND BETRAYAL

With the C'tan and the Necrons fighting as one, the Old Ones were now doomed to defeat. Glutted on the life force of the Necrontyr, the empowered C'tan were near unstoppable, and unleashed forces beyond comprehension. Planets were razed, suns extinguished and whole systems devoured by black holes called into being by the reality-warping powers of the star gods. Necron legions finally broached the webway and assailed the Old Ones in every corner of the galaxy. They brought under siege the fortresses of the Old Ones' allies, harvesting the life force of the defenders to feed their masters. Ultimately, beset by the implacable advance of the C'tan and the calamitous warp-spawned perils they had themselves mistakenly released, the Old Ones were defeated once and for all.

Throughout the final stages of the War in Heaven, Szarekh bided his time, waiting for the moment in which the C'tan would be vulnerable. Though the entire Necron race was his to command, he could not hope to oppose the C'tan at the height of their power. Even if he did, and somehow met with success, the Necrons would still then have to finish the War in Heaven alone. No, the Old Ones had to be defeated before the C'tan could be brought to account for the horror they had wrought. And so it was that, when the C'tan finally won their great war, their triumph was short-lived. With one hated enemy finally defeated, and the other spent from hard-fought victory, the

Silent King at last led the Necrons in revolt against the star gods.

In their arrogance, the C'tan did not realize their danger until it was too late. The Necrons focused the unimaginable energies of the living universe into weapons too powerful for even the C'tan to endure. Alas, the C'tan were immortal star-spawn, part of the fundamental fabric of actuality and impossible to destroy entirely. So was each C'tan instead sundered into thousands of fragments. Yet this was sufficient to the Silent King's goals. Indeed, he had known the C'tan's utter annihilation to be unachievable and had drawn his plans accordingly: each C'tan Shard was bound securely within the extra-dimensional space of a tesseract labyrinth, unable to escape. Though the cost of victory was high – millions had been killed as a consequence of rebellion, including all of the Triarch save the Silent King himself – the Necrons were once more in command of their own destiny.

Yet even with the defeat of the Old Ones and the C'tan alike, the Silent King saw that the time of the Necrons was over – for the moment, at least. The mantle of galactic dominion would soon pass to the Aeldari, a race who had fought alongside the Old Ones throughout the War in Heaven and had thus come to hate the Necrons and all their works. The Aeldari had survived where the Old Ones had not, and the Necrons, weakened during the overthrow of the C'tan, could not stand against them. Yet the Silent King knew that the time of the Aeldari would pass, as did the time of all flesh.

So it was that the Silent King ordered the remaining Necron cities to be transformed into great tomb complexes threaded with stasis-crypts. Let the Aeldari shape the galaxy for a time – they were but ephemeral, whilst the Necrons were eternal. The Silent King's final command to his people was that they must sleep for sixty million years but awake ready to rebuild all that they had lost, to restore the dynasties to their former glory. Thus was the Silent King's order given, and as the last tomb world sealed its vaults, he destroyed the command protocols by which he had controlled his people, for he knew he had failed them utterly. Without a backward glance, Szarekh, last of the Silent Kings, sailed into the blackness of intergalactic space, there to find whatever measure of solace or penance he could. Meanwhile, aeons passed, and the Necrons slept on…

# THE GREAT AWAKENING

None can say for sure how many tomb worlds entered the Great Sleep, but it is certain that a large number did not survive into the 41st Millennium. Technologically advanced though the Necrons were, to attempt a stasis-sleep of such scale was a great risk, even for them.

The Necrons slept for sixty million years, voicelessly waiting for their chance to complete the Silent King's final order – to restore the Necron dynasties to their former glory. As the centuries passed, ever more tomb worlds fell prey to malfunction or ill fortune. For many, the results were minor, such as a disruption to the operation of the tomb world's chronostat or revivification chambers, causing the inhabitants to awaken later than intended – but some tomb worlds suffered more calamitous events.

Cascade failures of stasis-crypts destroyed millions, if not billions, of dormant Necrons. Entire tomb worlds were destroyed by the retribution of marauding Aeldari warhosts, their defence systems overmatched by these ancient enemies. Others fell to the uncaring evolution of the galaxy itself: unstable planets crushed Necron strongholds slumbering at their hearts, supernovae consumed orbiting tomb worlds in their death throes, and everywhere, inquisitive life forms scrabbled over the bones of the Necron territories, causing more damage in their unthinking search for knowledge than the vengeful Aeldari ever could.

## RISING FROM OBLIVION

The awakening has been far from precise, and the Necrons have not arisen as one but in fitful starts over scattered millennia, like some gestalt sleeper rising from a troubled dream. Errors in circuitry and protocols ensured that a revivification destined to take place in the early years of the 41st Millennium actually began far earlier in a few cases, or has yet to occur at all in others. The very first of the tomb worlds to revive did so almost ten thousand years early, and bore witness to Mankind's Great Crusade sweeping across the galaxy. A handful stirred in time to see Nova Terra challenge the authority of the Golden Throne, or arose at the hour in which the Apostles of the Blind King waged their terrible wars. Some have never awoken. Even now, at the close of the 41st Millennium, billions of Necrons still slumber in their tombs beneath unknowing civilisations, silently awaiting the clarion call of destiny.

It is rare for a tomb world to awaken to full function swiftly. With but the slightest flaw in the revivification cycle, the engrammic pathway of a sleeper scatters and degrades. In most cases, these coalesce over time to restore identity and purpose, but it is a process that can take decades, or even centuries, and cannot be hurried. Sometimes recovery never occurs, and the sleeper is doomed forever to a mindless state.

There are thousands of tomb worlds scattered throughout the galaxy whose halls are thronged with shambling automatons, Necrons whose minds fled during hibernation, and whose bodies have been co-opted by a tomb world's master program in an attempt to bring some form of order to their existence. Other Necrons refer to such places as the Severed Worlds, and they loathe and fear their inhabitants in equal measure. None of this is to say that even an individual lucky enough to achieve a flawless revivification awakens alert and aware.

One of the hidden tyrannies of biotransference was how it entrenched the gulf between the rulers and the ruled, for there were not resources enough to provide all Necrontyr with bodies capable of retaining the full gamut of personality and awareness. Thus, as was ever the case, the very finest artificial bodies went to individuals of high rank: the phaerons and Overlords, and their Crypteks and nemesors. For the professional soldiery, the merely adequate was deemed appropriate. As for the common people, they received that which remained – comparatively crude armoured forms that were little more than prisons into which their lobotomised minds were placed. Numb to all joy and experience, they are bound solely to the will of their betters, their function meaningless without constant direction. Yet even here a tiny spark of self-awareness remains, enough only to torment the Necron with memories and echoes of the past it once knew. For these tortured creatures, death would be far preferable but, alas, they no longer have the wit to realise it.

## DOLMEN GATES

In the closing years of the War in Heaven, the tides began to shift when the Necrons finally gained access to the webway. The C'tan known as *Nyadra'zatha*, the Burning One, had long desired to carry his eldritch fires into that space beyond space, and so showed the Necrons how to breach its boundaries. Through a series of living stone portals known as the dolmen gates, the Necrons were finally able to turn the Old Ones' greatest weapon against them, vastly accelerating the end of the War in Heaven.

The portals offered by the dolmen gates are neither so stable, nor so controllable as those created by the ancient Aeldari to access the webway. In some curious fashion, the webway can detect when its environs have been breached by a dolmen gate and swiftly attempts to seal off the infected spur until the danger to its integrity has passed. As such, Necrons entering the webway must reach their destination quickly, lest the network itself bring about their destruction.

Aeons have passed since those times. The Old Ones are gone, and the webway itself has become a tangled and broken labyrinth. Many dolmen gates were lost or abandoned during the time of the Great Sleep, and many more were destroyed by the Aeldari. Those that remain grant access to but a small portion of the webway, much of that voluntarily sealed off by the Aeldari to prevent further contamination. Yet the webway is immeasurably vast, and even these sundered skeins allow the Necrons a mode of travel that far outpaces those of the younger races. It is well that this is so. As a race bereft of psykers, the Necrons are incapable of warp travel, and without access to the webway, they would be forced to rely once more on slow-voyaging stasis-ships, all but ending their ambition to re-establish their empire of old.

## UNSLEEPING DEFENCES

A tomb world is at its most vulnerable during the revivification process. The colossal amounts of energy generated are detectable across great distances, and are an irresistible lure to the inquisitive and acquisitive alike. In these early stages, it is unlikely that the army of a tomb world proper will have awoken to full function, so defence lies in the hands of the Necrons' servitor robots – the Canoptek Spyders, Scarabs and Wraiths.

Initially, these defenders will be directed by the tomb world's master program, whose complex decision matrix allows it to calculate an efficient response to any perceived threat. As the threat level rises, so too does the intensity of the master program's countermeasures, prioritising the activation of the tomb world's defences and the revivification of its armies according to the situation at hand. If all goes well, the master program's actions will be sufficient to drive out the invader, or at least stall their ingress until the first legions have awoken – at which point the master program surrenders command to the tomb world's nobles.

When a large population centre of a younger race has evolved or expanded close to a tomb world, the encoded programming delves deep into its archives and armouries in order to conduct an aggressive defence. Such tomb worlds are the ones that have expanded their spheres of influence most rapidly, for its rulers have awakened to find their full military might already mobilised and awaiting command. Indeed, the speed with which many tomb worlds of the Sautekh Dynasty have recovered lost territory is chiefly attributable to the ultimately doomed wave of Uluméathi colonies established on their coreworlds during late M39.

## A RETURN TO POWER

To external observers, the behaviour of awoken tomb worlds must seem inconsistent almost to the point of randomness. Some Necron Lords send diplomatic emissaries to other worlds, negotiating for the return of lost territories and artefacts, or cast off into the stars, searching for distant tomb worlds not yet awoken. Others focus attention inwards, avoiding unnecessary conflict with alien races to pursue internal politics or oversee the rebuilding of their planet to glory.

The vast majority of tomb worlds, however, take a more aggressive tack, launching resource raids, planetary invasions or full-blown genocidal purges. Yet even here, it is impossible to predict the precise form these deeds will take. Sometimes the Necrons attack in the full panoply and spectacle of honourable war, rigorously applying their ancient codes of battle. At others, every possible underhanded tactic is employed, from piracy and deception, to assassination and fomentation. On occasion, the campaign is less a martial action than a systematic extermination, the swatting of lesser life forms as they themselves would swat insects.

All of these acts, diverse though they are in scope and method, are directed towards a single common goal: the restoration of the Necron dynasties. Yet, with the Triarch long gone and huge numbers of tomb worlds lying desolate or dormant, there can be no galaxy-wide coordination, no grand strategy that will bring about Necron ascendancy. Instead, each tomb world's ruler must fend for himself, pursuing whatever course he deems most suited to the circumstance. For some, this is the domination of nearby threats and the sowing of terror on alien worlds. For others, it might be the recovery of cultural treasures, the stockpiling of raw materials

for campaigns yet to come, or even the search for an organic species whose bodies might be suitable vessels for Necron minds, thus finally ending the curse of biotransference. Indeed, this last matter – the apotheosis from machine to living being – is the key motivating factor for many Necron nobles, for its possibility weighed heavily on the Silent King's mind at the moment of his final command.

All this is further complicated by the fact that the departure of the Silent King and the dissolution of the Triarch left no clear succession. As a result, the rulers of many tomb worlds see an opportunity not only to restore the dynasties of old, but also to improve their standing within the wider Necron hierarchy. The motives of Necron nobles are often muddied by the pursuit of personal power, making accurate divination of an individual's intentions – and therefore of the campaigns conducted by his legions – an almost impossible task.

> 'ADVERSARY, KNOW THAT YOUR SQUALID COLONY RESTS UPON THE RIGHTFUL CROWNWORLD OF THE NOVOKH DYNASTY. KNOW ALSO THAT WHILST YOUR PRESENCE CANNOT BE TOLERATED, WE ARE BOUND BY CODE OF HONOUR TO ALLOW YOU OPPORTUNITY TO WITHDRAW. YOU ARE THEREFORE GRANTED ONE SOLAR MONTH, COMMENCING AT TERMINATION OF THIS TRANSMISSION, TO REMOVE ALL TRACE OF YOUR PRESENCE. IF YOU FAIL TO ACCEPT THIS GENEROUS OFFER, MY ARMIES SHALL CONCLUDE THESE NEGOTIATIONS. WE ADVISE YOU NOT TO MISTAKE HONOURABLE WARNING FOR LACK OF RESOLVE.'
>
> *- Ultimatum received by Governor Mendican Harrow of hive world Dhol VI*

## CONTESTED DOMINION

With the opening of the Great Rift, the rate at which tomb worlds are being roused has increased drastically. Unsleeping sentinels placed on Necron worlds thousands of millennia ago have observed the auroral rent in the galactic plane. Driven by ancient protocols, these automata initiate the processes of revivification, and the legions slumbering beneath the sands are once more imparted with a simulacrum of life.

Like all tomb worlds, those recently awakened are replete with the resources most precious to the Necrons – minerals and esoteric substances used in their most powerful technomantic creations. The most valued of these resources is noctilith, known in Low Gothic as blackstone. It is through blackstone that the Necrons are able to create their star-spanning tetrahedral zones of stable space, perfectly ordered tracts of reality that are resistant to the warping influences of Chaos.

But over the long years in which the Necrons slept, others have been drawn to the raw wealth of their tomb worlds. The Adeptus Mechanicus, in particular, founded many quarries upon these mineral-rich planets, layering their surfaces with rockcrete hab-domes and vast manufactorums. Their Tech-Priests experimented endlessly on the blackstone they found, and whilst never tapping its true potential, they harvested much of it for their own arcane devices. Now the Necrons are rising from beneath the foundations of these settlements. Their glowing eyes are fixed on the wealth that has been stolen from them, and they mercilessly eradicate those who have unknowingly encroached upon their domain.

# THE NECRON DYNASTIES

Even in life, the Necrontyr civilisation was one of strict protocol and process, governed by nobles whose rule was absolute. This rigid hierarchy became more entrenched during the transition from flesh to machine, and the awakening Necron civilisation is far more complex and stratified than the one that once ruled the galaxy.

## SAUTEKH DYNASTY

In the times before biotransference, the Sautekh Dynasty was ranked third most powerful of all the royal dynasties. Through chance or design, many of the Sautekh coreworlds survived the aeons far better than those of their rivals. Now, this dynasty is far stronger than any other, and is the most mercilessly efficient in enacting each new wave of expansion. Both the Imperium of Mankind and, more recently, the T'au Empire have suffered greatly at the hands of the Sautekh Dynasty's conquering armies, as Imotekh pushes ever further into the Eastern Fringe.

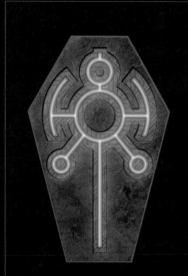

## CHARNOVOKH DYNASTY

Much of the territory once ruled by the Charnovokh Dynasty lies far to the galactic southeast. Many of its dormant tomb worlds were devoured by Hive Fleet Behemoth, and countless others have been ravaged during the Imperium's counter-attacks against the Tyranids. Only the strongest have survived, so the forces of the Charnovokh Dynasty are disparate but utterly formidable.

## NEPHREKH DYNASTY

The masters of the Nephrekh Dynasty seek not to reverse biotransference and become bodies of flesh and blood, but to transform into creatures of pure light. The Nephrekh's recent attempts to pierce the darkness of the Cicatrix Maledictum and extend the range of their translocation beams by utilising immense celestial engines have been impeded by the Thousand Sons – the Sons of Magnus seek to claim these wonders as their own.

## THOKT DYNASTY

The Thokt Dynasty has staked its claim in the wilderness of the Segmentum Pacificus for good reason. By harnessing the energies of the void rifts that surround its coreworlds, the Thokt not only give themselves a near-limitless source of energy, but also surround themselves with such a potent aura of baleful radiation that those living creatures near them swiftly weaken, sicken and ultimately die.

## MEPHRIT DYNASTY

The Mephrit Dynasty has no phaeron to govern it, for their crownworld was lost to a Hrud infestation during the Great Sleep. Many of its Overlords now compete for prominence, hoping to establish the position of phaeron. Masters of star-killing weaponry, the Mephrit have recently turned these destructive technologies upon their hated foes, the Aeldari, burning the life from several Exodite worlds and claiming the ashen remains as their own. Craftworlds Alaitoc and Saim-Hann have united in an attempt to push back the Mephrit's relentless advance.

## NOVOKH DYNASTY

The warlike Novokh remember the rites of blooding undertaken during the ancient Wars of Secession, where their warriors would daub their faces and arms in the blood of those they slew. The dynasty's Lords have fully indulged their lust for combat and conquest amidst the madness of the Imperium Nihilus, claiming worlds from both the Imperium of Mankind and the armies of Chaos in a series of bloody campaigns.

## OGDOBEKH DYNASTY

The Ogdobekh Dynasty's tomb worlds were well prepared for the Great Sleep, every one outfitted with backup systems and untold legions of Canoptek constructs to watch over them. The dynasty is fortunate that it possesses such impressive reserves, for its domain reaches into the Segmentum Solar, near to the heart of the Imperium's power. The Ogdobekh are on a constant war footing against the armies of Humanity.

## NIHILAKH DYNASTY

The Nihilakh have always guarded the borders of their ancient lands with ferocious zeal. Yet since the Great Rift opened, the dynasty's legions have been seen abroad with increasing regularity, actively hunting the forces of Chaos. Stranger still, the Nihilakh appear to have cordoned off a large sector of space within their domain, and their billions of slaves work tirelessly to erect enormous, geometrically arranged monuments.

# THE AWAKENING EMPIRE

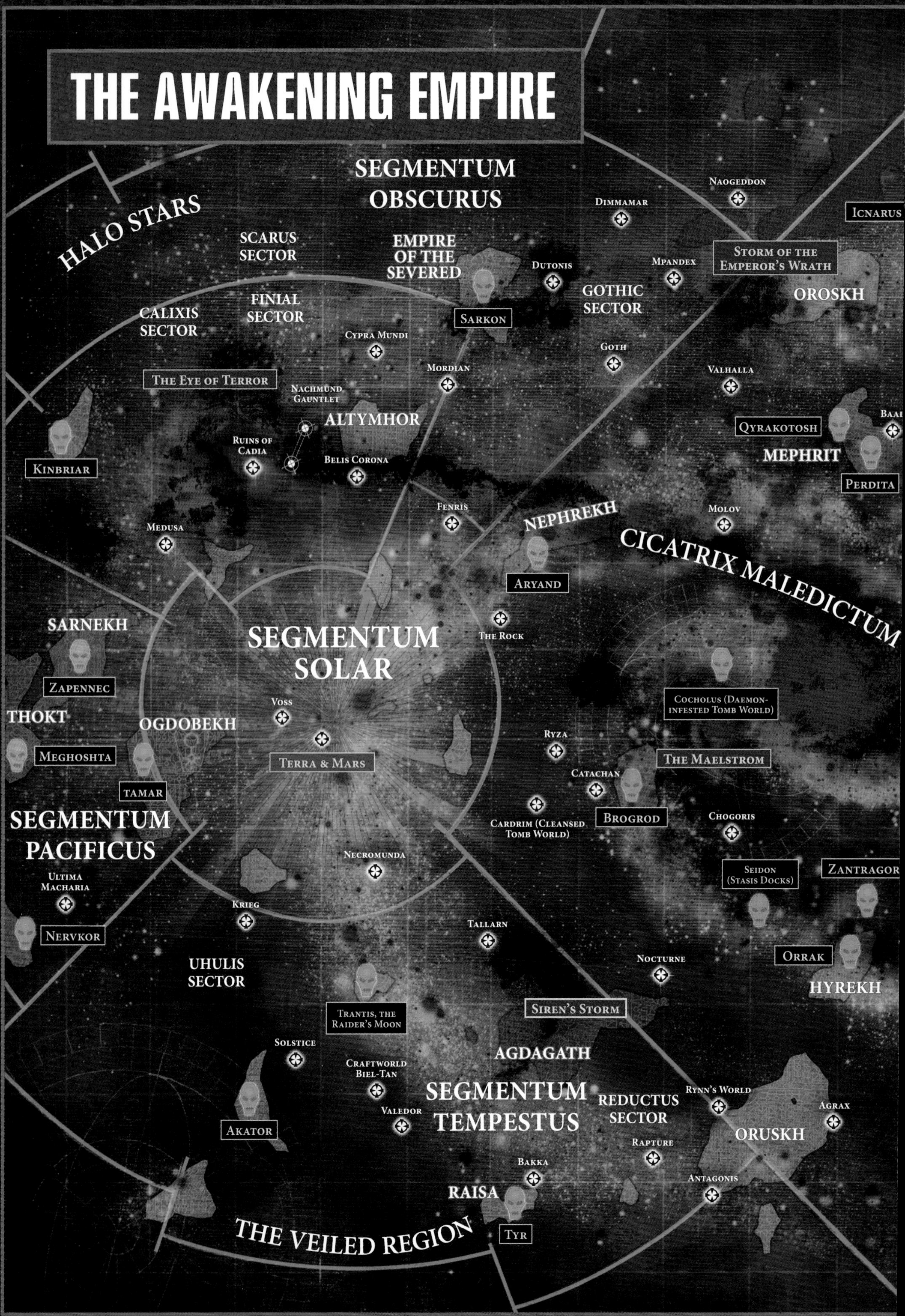

SEGMENTUM OBSCURUS

HALO STARS

NAOGEDDON

DIMMAMAR

ICNARUS

SCARUS SECTOR

EMPIRE OF THE SEVERED

DUTONIS

MPANDEX

STORM OF THE EMPEROR'S WRATH

OROSKH

CALIXIS SECTOR

FINIAL SECTOR

GOTHIC SECTOR

SARKON

CYPRA MUNDI

GOTH

VALHALLA

THE EYE OF TERROR

MORDIAN

QYRAKOTOSH

BAAL

NACHMUND GAUNTLET

ALTYMHOR

MEPHRIT

RUINS OF CADIA

BELIS CORONA

PERDITA

KINBRIAR

FENRIS

NEPHREKH

MOLOV

MEDUSA

CICATRIX MALEDICTUM

ARYAND

SARNEKH

SEGMENTUM SOLAR

THE ROCK

ZAPENNEC

VOSS

COCHOLUS (DAEMON-INFESTED TOMB WORLD)

THOKT

OGDOBEKH

TERRA & MARS

RYZA

THE MAELSTROM

MEGHOSHTA

CATACHAN

TAMAR

CARDRIM (CLEANSED TOMB WORLD)

BROGROD

CHOGORIS

SEGMENTUM PACIFICUS

NECROMUNDA

SEIDON (STASIS DOCKS)

ZANTRAGOR

ULTIMA MACHARIA

KRIEG

TALLARN

NERVKOR

ORRAK

NOCTURNE

UHULIS SECTOR

HYREKH

TRANTIS, THE RAIDER'S MOON

SIREN'S STORM

SOLSTICE

AGDAGATH

RYNN'S WORLD

CRAFTWORLD BIEL-TAN

SEGMENTUM TEMPESTUS

REDUCTUS SECTOR

AGRAX

VALEDOR

ORUSKH

AKATOR

RAPTURE

BAKKA

ANTAGONIS

RAISA

TYR

THE VEILED REGION

OCCULID

MALFACTUS

SOLITUDE

...TUN

NOVOKH

DHOL VI

DRAVEN

ANGELIS

BONE KINGDOM
OF DRAZAK

DESPERATION

ASTRO TELEPATHIC DUCT

NEXUS III
ASTRO STATION

ORUSCAR

SOMNIUM STARS

KARDENATH

ULTIMA
SEGMENTUM

NAGATHAR

THANATOS

HEXOS

AVARRIS

...NEKTHYST

GIDRIM

TRIPLEX
PHALL

SAUTEKH

MOEBIUS
(THE TWISTED
CATACOMB)

ARRYNMAROK

TEMPORARY
RIFT
CORRIDOR

VENGEANCE

YMGA MONOLITH

DYVANAKH

THE EASTERN FRINGE

TRAKONN

MANDRAGORA

SARLOK

RITHCARIN

SEKEMTAR

HADEX ANOMALY

...ARADON
...ECTOR

MEDUSA VII

CRAFTWORLD
ALAITOC

MACRAGGE

CHARNOVOKH

...LEMNACE

DAMNOS

GHEDEN

AMONTEP II

...IHILAKH

BARDIC

Scattered throughout the vast celestial wilderness slumber the worlds of the impossibly ancient Necron Empire. Ignorant of the armies that lie beneath their feet, the young races built their civilisations upon the tombs of the old. The Imperium, always swift to consider itself the ruler of the galaxy, spread across the stars, unaware that there was another that had already laid claim to that title. Now, after millions of years locked in the timeless embrace of their stasis-crypts, the Necron Empire is stirring once more.

So far, but the barest fraction of Necron tomb worlds have roused to terrible life, but with every passing year the number grows. Each time a Necron planet is restored a cascade is triggered, and the dormant tomb worlds of nearby systems will soon follow. Vast solar empires are carved anew from the burning civilisations and fallen armies of the Necrons' enemies. Piece by piece, the fragments of the dynastic domains are being drawn together, seditious Overlords and vengeful phaerons searing the stars clean for the return of their kingdoms.

What the Imperium cannot know is that, should the Necrons ever fully wake and unite, they would face a foe as numerous as themselves. For now, the galaxy has had but a taste of the dynasties' destructive potential, and it is fortunate for their foes that the Necrons remain divided by madness and conflicting agendas. However, these are but the first stumbling steps of a giant as it gathers pace, and even now powerful leaders like Anrakyr the Traveller, Imotekh the Stormlord and the Silent King are uniting their people under a common cause.

KEY

*Active Tomb World*

*Dormant Tomb World*

*Crownworld*

*Dynastic Territories*

*Areas of Interest*

# DOMAIN OF THE PHAERONS

The Necrons wage war as they did in times of old – their immortal phaerons casting their armies out into the great sea of stars to conquer the worlds of the unworthy. Armies of lockstep legions and contemptuous generals descend upon their foes, honouring their ancient oaths of fealty with the death of worlds and the blood of civilisations.

Aeons ago, the Necron Empire was a tapestry of interlocking dynasties that stretched across the stars. Each dynasty spread out around its crownworld like planets orbiting a sun, those close to the light of the phaeron's rule basking in his glory. The crownworld was the phaeron's seat of power, and the wealth of its vassal planets flowed towards it like an incoming tide. Secondary to the crownworld were the coreworlds, each one ruled by a Lord or Overlord of the phaeron, vying among themselves for the favour of their master. However, the further one travelled from the crownworld, the more weakly its influence could be felt. The outermost planets, known as fringeworlds, were mere colonies that knew little of their phaeron's beneficence.

Like the hierarchy of Necron planets, the armies of the tomb worlds are each beholden to their betters just as each noble is a part of his phaeron's empire. Similarly, the Necron courts form political webs centred around the regent of each tomb world. Crypteks create and maintain the Necrons' esoteric machinery, while the Triarch Praetorians take their place as enforcers for the Silent King. Under these, like the clawed limbs of the phaeron, are the twin arms of the Necron soldiery and his engines of war.

The master of a tomb world will rely upon his Warriors, Immortals and Tomb Blades to be the hard edge of his will, whereas Lychguard and Deathmarks are specialists used more sparingly, and only against those considered worthy of their attention. By contrast, potent machines of destruction such as the Monolith and Doomsday Ark are reserved for wars of annihilation or extreme enemy resistance, where their prodigious firepower can sweep away their foes in a blaze of matter-tearing energy.

Beneath a phaeron's teeming ranks of soldiery and forbidding techno-armoury are the auxiliaries – those more akin to allies than true warriors of the dynasty. Counted among these are the Destroyer Cults and Flayed One packs. Largely untrustworthy and often dangerously insane, Destroyers are tolerated only for the havoc they wreak in battle. Likewise, Flayed Ones are a curse that seems to follow the legions to war, regardless of whether they are called upon or not. Finally, below even these twisted misfits of the Necron Empire are the shackled shards of the C'tan. In spite of their world-splitting powers, it gives the phaerons great pleasure to know that the star gods are lesser in status than even the least of their slaves.

## Tomb World Assets
- Tomb World Flagship
- Tomb World Capital Ship
- Tomb Ship Squadrons
- Secondary Escort Squadrons
- C'tan Shards
- Auxiliary Forces
- Orbital Defences
- Doomsday Weapons

## Tesserarion Assets
- Tesserarion Flagship
- Planetary Assault Craft and Drop Ships
- Escort Squadrons
- Super-heavy Cohorts

## Decurion Assets
- Crypteks
- Triarch Praetorians
- Tomb Blades
- Ghost Arks
- Flayed One Packs
- Attack Craft
- Deathmarks
- War Engines
- Super-heavy assets
- Destroyers
- Canoptek Scarabs

## Legion Assets
- Cruisers
- Escorts
- Cryptek Conclaves
- Attack Craft Squadrons
- Super-heavy Phalanxes
- Triarch Judicator Battalions
- Deathmark Guilds
- Destroyer Cults
- Flayer Cults
- War Engine Cohorts
- Canoptek Swarms

*'Let me tell you of my future. My hand will reach out into the stars, reshaping the galaxy into a place of order and unity. Under my reign, the kingdoms of old shall live again, reborn to an age of power and glory the like of which you can only imagine. I will rule every planet touched by the light of this star and, even in the darkness beyond, my name will be whispered with fear and respect.*

*Your future, by contrast, is looking less than glorious – you will not be reaching out your hand to anything ever again, I think. Embrace the pain and humiliation of its loss, so that you may better learn the lessons of this defeat. Learn them well enough, and you may even be reborn as an enemy worthy of my attention. A hand is a measly price for such a gift, is it not?'*

*- Imotekh the Stormlord to Eldorath Starbane,*
*in the wake of the Siege of Somonor*

## TOMB WORLD
### Tomb World Command
**Regent** (Primary Overlord)
**Regent's Court** (Overlords, Lords and Crypteks)
**Vargard** (Overlord)
**Lychguard** (Bodyguard to the Nemesor)

| 2nd Tesserarion | 3rd Tesserarion | 4th Tesserarion | 5th Tesserarion etc. |
|---|---|---|---|

## 1ST TESSERARION
### Tesserarion Command
**Nemesor** (Overlord)
**Nemesor's Court** (Bodyguards and advisors to the Nemesor)
**Lychguard**

| 2nd Decurion | 3rd Decurion | 4th Decurion | 5th Decurion etc. |
|---|---|---|---|

## 1ST DECURION
### Decurion Command
**Nemesor** (Overlord)
**Nemesor's Court** (Overlord and Cryptek advisors to the Nemesor)
**Vargard** (Lord)

| 2nd Legion | 3rd Legion | 4th Legion | 5th Legion etc. |
|---|---|---|---|

## 1ST LEGION
### Legion Command
**Overlord**
**Overlord's Court** (Overlord, Lord and Cryptek advisors to the Overlord)

## 1ST COHORT
**Vargard** (Lord)
1st Phalanx
2nd Phalanx
3rd Phalanx
4th Phalanx
5th Phalanx

## 2ND COHORT
**Vargard** (Lord)
6th Phalanx
7th Phalanx
8th Phalanx
9th Phalanx
10th Phalanx

Nominally legions number ten phalanxes, each consisting of ten Necrons. These are divided into two cohorts, each led by a vargard detached from the nemesor's Royal Court. Legions may consist of Warriors, Immortals, rarer units such as Lychguard or Deathmarks, or whichever combination of these units appeals to their Overlord.

# DYNASTIC MARKINGS

Necrons are haunted by the echoes of their proud militaristic past, and consequently retain the pageantry of their once-great empire. Though the death of stars and the destruction of worlds has changed the celestial landscape of the Necron Empire, these fragments of its past live on, inspiring fear and dread in the lesser races.

Necron Warriors bear the colours of their dynasty, and any other heraldry their Overlord sees fit to bestow upon them. Sautekh Warriors employ the cold silver and electric green used by their phaeron, Imotekh.

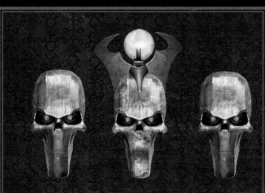

Unfeeling and disposable, Necron Warriors typically bear only the colours of their dynasty and tomb world. A Lychguard's golden death mask, by contrast, indicates its esteemed position within a Necron Overlord's bodyguard retinue.

The ankh upon a Necron Warrior's chest binds it to the Triarch and shows that it has a place within the Necron Empire. However, it also acts as a mark of personal ownership. Legions bear the colours of their Lords and Overlords upon the ankh, with more ostentatious markings signifying a more important master. The use of gold in the ankh or cartouche is a mark of high honour afforded to the personal legions of a tomb world's ruler.

The living-metal form of a Necron is a marvel of ancient science. It can bear myriad colours, textures and markings, and the Necrons of two dynasties are seldom alike. Some appear forged from burnished silvered steel, their hard shells untarnished by age. Others look like they have been cast from ceramics, stone or even glass, hinting at the strange technologies used to create them. Over these unyielding surfaces, the symbols and colours of the dynasties proudly proclaim the warriors' allegiance.

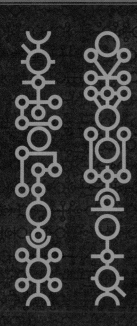

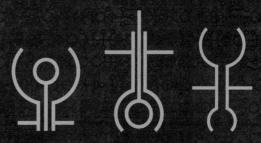

The large flat panels of a Monolith's hull often display the dynastic markings of its owner, his personal glyphs appearing alongside other hieroglyphs.

A tomb world's war machines often display hieroglyphs in the Necron language. These may be battle honours, markings of ownership, or proclamations of the owner's power.

A Tomb Blade's pilot will display his allegiance in the colours of his chest ankh. Tomb Blades usually bear further glyphs denoting their designated roles within their flight's attack pattern, which are applied to the living-metal bodywork of their craft.

## ANKH OF THE TRIARCH

All Necrons bear the mark of the Triarch, a brand upon their living-metal skin that binds them to their race. The Triarch were a triumvirate of phaerons that ruled the Necrons, and the one known as the Silent King was the greatest of the three. In the 41st Millennium, the absence of the Silent King and the long years of the Great Sleep have transformed the Ankh of the Triarch into a reminder of faded glory. Some nobles still see it as the foundation of the Necron Empire, while for others it is merely an echo of a long-dead age. However, the Ankh remains a ubiquitous symbol of the Necrons, and even those who have lost faith in its power still bear it on a cartouche adorning their torso. Each dynasty will vary the colours of the Ankh and cartouche to match those of their phaeron. However, despite these cosmetic alterations, the shape of the Ankh remains unchanged, each exacting curve and line perfectly reproduced upon the Necrons' chests.

Each dynasty also possesses its own glyphs, which are variations on the Ankh that identify its soldiers as part of a particular phaeron's armies. These symbols are sometimes worn alongside the Ankh of the Triarch, but are usually secondary in size and placement, mirroring the ancient relationship between the phaeron and the Triarch. Lesser soldiery are rarely granted the distinction of bearing these dynastic symbols on their bodies in full, as such ranks are generally considered unworthy of the honour – instead, elements of the dynastic glyph are used to identify individual phalanxes.

# SAUTEKH DYNASTY

## THE IMPLACABLE TEMPEST

The Sautekh Dynasty is known for two things above all others – the merciless efficiency with which they disassemble the armies of their foes, and the byzantine hierarchy that governs them. With every year the Sautekh absorb, annex or conquer new worlds and lesser dynasties, each fresh acquisition made a shining cog in their silvered machinery of destruction.

Like a steel claw bursting from the heart of the galaxy, the Sautekh Dynasty emerged from the Great Sleep in a storm of death and destruction. Unified under the iron will of Imotekh the Stormlord, the Sautekh wield a power and purpose like no other dynasty. From their crownworld of Mandragora, the implacable legions of Imotekh spread out across the stars, bringing more and more worlds under the rule of their phaeron. Even other Necron dynasties bow down to the power of the Sautekh, joining the ranks of the Stormlord's armies. Overlord Naszar of the Sekemtar, Celestium Emriit of the Horth and Overlord Szaron of the Arrynmarok have all pledged themselves to Imotekh's cause, hungry for a piece of the domain he is carving from the stars.

Resplendent in burnished silver and cold emerald, the legions of the Sautekh have brought to heel scores of worlds across the Eastern Fringe. By the light of burning civilisations, Imotekh's armies march relentlessly on, driven by the Stormlord's dreams of conquest and reunification. It is Imotekh's will that his people be forged anew, and that he rise to rule all Necrons. At first, the phaeron's desire was born of necessity, as he awoke to find his tomb world wracked by infighting. Rather than pick sides, the Stormlord dispatched his rivals and seized power for himself. Now, as the influence of the Sautekh waxes, so too does that of Imotekh, and the former nemesor sees himself as the architect of the Necrons' return to primacy.

As the most numerous of the arisen Necron dynasties, it is the Sautekh that have been encountered most frequently by other races. To the Imperium, the dynasty has become synonymous with the Necrons, and it is erroneously believed by many that they represent the alien race as a whole, with all other dynasties being mere offshoots of the Sautekh. The T'au see the dynasty as representatives of an emergent power, and seek as ever to form allegiances before resorting to all-out war. To the Aeldari, the Stormlord represents the greatest threat posed by the Necrons, for they know that should he realise his ambitions, the horrors of a bygone age will once more return to the galaxy.

Imotekh himself understands that the enemies of the Sautekh are many and powerful – perhaps too many to defeat with force of arms alone. As such, the master strategist uses other weapons to bring the galaxy under his control. As he sweeps across the stars, a shadow of terror passes before him; the worlds he plans to conquer are wracked by violent storms and scorched by unnatural lightning. Armies that march out to meet the Stormlord disappear into his shadow, and so the legend of terror grows.

On their dark reputation alone have systems surrendered to the Sautekh, preferring a life as slaves of the Necrons to annihilation at the hands of their legions. So it is that the relentless expansion of the Sautekh continues, and Imotekh takes another step towards total domination.

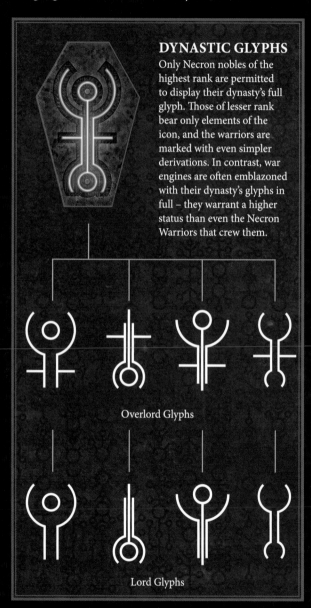

### DYNASTIC GLYPHS

Only Necron nobles of the highest rank are permitted to display their dynasty's full glyph. Those of lesser rank bear only elements of the icon, and the warriors are marked with even simpler derivations. In contrast, war engines are often emblazoned with their dynasty's glyphs in full – they warrant a higher status than even the Necron Warriors that crew them.

Overlord Glyphs

Lord Glyphs

### PHALANX GLYPHS

Units of lesser warriors and war machines amongst a legion are marked with a primary element of their dynasty's glyph. The simplicity of these markings speaks of their low status in the hierarchy of the Necrons. As these elements derive from the dynasty's symbol, the same glyphs will be used by legions from different tomb worlds within a dynasty, the legions' ownership indicted by the colours displayed in the Ankh of the Triarch.

Immortal phalanxes bear the same markings as Necron Warriors, though many also display an honorific band upon their brow to reflect their status.

Clad in royal regalia, Lychguard echo the grandeur of their lords. Golden head-crests and segmented tabards make these warriors stand out from the common soldiery.

A particularly favoured phalanx of Immortals might display the colours of their phaeron. This can either mean the soldiers are part of the phaeron's personal legion or are operating under the auspices of one of his most trusted Overlords.

Immortals wear the Ankh of the Triarch with pride, their warrior minds recognising the symbol of their ancient empire. As with their lesser brethren, Immortals bear the colours of their Lord and Overlord upon their ankhs. These two Immortals display the marks of Overlord Zendrik and Azdrakh respectively.

# MEPHRIT DYNASTY

## THE SOLAR REAPERS

**The Mephrit Dynasty has a history of star-killing grandeur and a talent for annihilation through fire. Though much of their glory has been lost, they are still able to harness and deploy extremely powerful energies.**

Pitiless planet killers, the Mephrit were the solar executioners of the War in Heaven. Stars withered and died under the meticulous attention of their Crypteks, while their phaerons condemned entire systems to death through hyper-accelerated supernovae. Often, it would be the legions of the Mephrit that the Silent King summoned when a race or planet proved especially defiant, as the dynasty had proved its talent for extermination time and again. Many of the other phaerons considered the Mephrit's methods excessive or distasteful by the ancient codes of warfare. Yet the dynasty's victories spoke for themselves, and they swiftly rose in power and prominence. Unfortunately, the slow march of the aeons and the Great Sleep has left the Mephrit's splendour

faded and tattered. The world-rending weapons for which they were once famous are lost to the void or fallen into disrepair, while many of their coreworlds are no more. Perhaps most disastrous of all for the Mephrit was the loss of their phaeron, Khyrek the Eternal, who was obliterated along with the dynasty's crownworld by Aeldari assassins. In the power vacuum left by their master's demise, many of the Mephrit's Overlords cling to the past, but there are those who look to future conquests. Among them, Zarathusa the Ineffable gazes upon the ruins of his system and covets the power he once wielded. Guiding his legions, he has set off on a crusade of reclamation. Soon, the galaxy will learn to fear the Mephrit as it did in days of old.

The Mephrit's dynastic icon is based upon the constellation formed around their crownworld's star, each spar pointing to a vassal sun or shield system.

The Mephrit's mastery of exotic energies is boldly displayed in the ranks of their soldiery; the captive light of suns burns within all of the weapons they unleash upon their foes, making the Mephrit instantly recognisable.

Overlord Glyphs

Lord Glyphs

Phalanx Glyphs

The Mephrit have no phaeron to govern them, and their crownworld was lost during the Great Sleep. Now, the Overlords of the dynasty compete for leadership, and many have enhanced their personal glyphs to reflect their self-elevated status. Regardless of how exceptional each claimant believes himself to be, all such lords use weaponry with the same distinctive energy emissions.

# NEPHREKH DYNASTY

### THE BRINGERS OF DAWN

**The Nephrekh are a dynasty consumed with showing their mastery over light itself. Their metal bodies can be converted to beams of pure energy, becoming one with the stars.**

The trinary suns of the Nephrekh crownworld glow golden upon the mantles of its legions. Rich in the solar wealth of scores of systems, the Nephrekh's worlds cluster around a dense concentration of stars, their radiant brilliance filling the skies with a near-limitless supply of energy. From this golden chalice of flame the Nephrekh drink deep, channelling its forces into translocation beams so powerful they can lead their armies from one system to another at the speed of light.

Phaeron Sylphek, like so many others, emerged from his long hyperstasis within his crownworld with his personality degraded to the edge of madness. He has become consumed by an obsession with the stars themselves, announcing to his bemused court that he wished to drape himself in their molten glory. To placate their lord, the Crypteks of the Nephrekh crafted Sylphek a skin of living metagold that can turn to pure light through advanced hyperalchemical processes – the phaeron has since seen himself as a celestial deity given bodily form. The 'golden form' is a gift Sylphek has since shared with his trusted servants. The dynasty's high-ranking Overlords can be temporarily transformed into living light, while even the lowliest Nephrekh warriors can activate traces of metagold within their metal bodies in order to shift and stutter across open ground at frightening speed. The secret to making this process permanent yet eludes the Nephrekh, but they have bent their formidable resources towards solving the conundrum.

At the centre of the Nephrekh's dynastic glyph are three overlapping circles representing the three stars of its crownworld.

The Nephrekh Dynasty's lowly warriors wear burnished gold colours, a pale imitation of their master's transcendent majesty that nonetheless looks striking and imposing when these soulless legions march to battle.

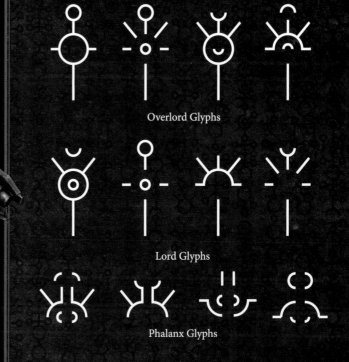

Overlord Glyphs

Lord Glyphs

Phalanx Glyphs

The glyphs of the Nephrekh aristocracy all contain some echo of the crownworld's trinary stars, often with branching lines to indicate the spreading of its magnificent light out into the wider galaxy. It is the desire of Phaeron Sylphek that one day every planet in the galaxy will look up into the skies and witness his brilliant radiance.

# NIHILAKH DYNASTY

## THE SENTINELS OF ETERNITY

**Regal and glorious in battle, the Nihilakh are fiercely territorial. Only at the close of the 41st Millennium have they turned their attention outwards, planning a new campaign of slow and relentless expansion.**

Woe to the army that trespasses upon the domains of the Nihilakh. In times of antiquity, the dynasty built vast treasure worlds filled with wealth plundered from a thousand civilisations. When the Nihilakh awoke from hibernation it was to find their once-mighty realm in ruins. Looking inwards, the dynasty gathered what strength they still possessed to their crownworld, Gheden. Now, they jealously guard the remaining wonders of their empire, shoring up their borders against all intrusion. The dynasty's Crypteks have recently begun the construction of strange monolithic arrangements along the frontier of Nihilakh space, though what purpose these creations serve is as yet unclear.

It is said that the splendours of the Nihilakh treasure houses eclipse those of all other dynasties combined, and their armaments attest to this. Arrogant and proud, the dynasty's Overlords ensure that none forget the great wealth of their people, nor the military strength that comes from it. They have their Crypteks work precious turquoise and jewels into the armour of the legions, and often carry prized relics into battle, borne upon their war engines as reminders of their ancient triumphs and glory.

Greatest among the dynasty's treasures is the Yyth Seer – the preserved head of an alien prophet who was the last of its race. Using neurographic resonators to peer into the prophet's mind, the Overlords have witnessed the future of their race. It has to be a future of unavoidable conflict, for the Nihilakh are gathering their legions for war.

The Nihilakh favour a strict military hierarchy; their phalanx markings are simplified versions of the overarching dynastic glyph.

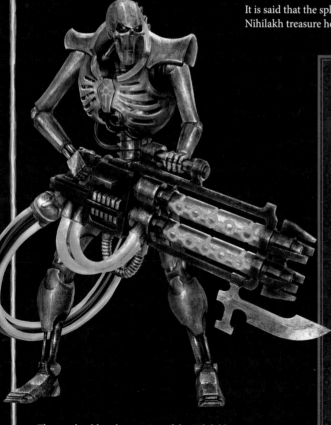

The regal gold and turquoise of the Nihilakh are worn not just by its highest-ranking members, but also its warriors, for its Overlords would find it distasteful to wage war with weapons that did not in some way proclaim their considerable wealth.

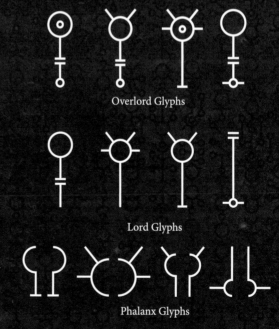

Overlord Glyphs

Lord Glyphs

Phalanx Glyphs

The Overlords and Lords of Nihilakh wear personal glyphs reflecting a segment of their dynasty's icon – only the phaeron is permitted to bear the icon in its entirety. Often, this personal symbol will signify the part of his dynasty's domain that the lord presides over. On lesser warriors, these glyphs are worn in gold upon turquoise; on more valued servants these colours are reversed.

# NOVOKH DYNASTY

## THE CRIMSON REAPERS

**The Novokh Dynasty has been slow to awaken, but with every new and bloody war, its resurgence accelerates. Its warriors are invigorated by the act of bloodshed: for them, the mark of success is a deep and livid red.**

Initially, a Novokh phalanx will go to the front line with a slow and plodding gait. When the close-range killing begins, however, it harnesses the flickering memories of the ancient blood rituals it once performed. As the gore of the foe splashes across their carapaces and skull-like masks, they seem to come more and more alive until they are fighting with unnatural vigour and determination.

The Novokh Dynasty has found a rising star in the form of Overlord Galmakh, the Moon Killer. Galmakh gained considerable fame before the Great Sleep with his tactic of destroying moons, thereby disrupting the gravity of worlds that defied him. At the heart of Galmakh's armies is the Crimson God, a C'tan Shard enslaved by the Novokh

Dynasty millennia ago. The shard is commanded at all times by the redoubtable Overlord known as the Crimson King. An unwilling vassal, the C'tan drifts ominously across the battlefield, meting out destruction with its incredible powers, but never quite in the way that the Crimson King would wish for.

Recent wars have seen the Novokh Dynasty ranged against the anarchic might of the greenskins, whose ceaseless rampage across the stars poses a dire threat to the Novokh's crownworld of Dhol VI. More than one Warboss has been utterly erased from existence by the Crimson God, leaving the Orks utterly baffled as they try to recall who it was they were following into battle mere moments ago.

The Novokh glyph reflects the core system cluster and its six wars of conquest. Simpler glyphs often reflect young or aggressively expansionist dynasties.

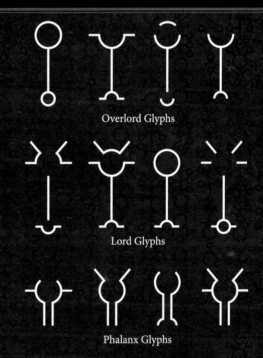

Overlord Glyphs

Lord Glyphs

Phalanx Glyphs

The Overlords and Lords of the Novokh wear a circular glyph to represent their crownworld, but will adapt this simple symbol with personal flourishes to represent particularly glorious victories or memorable duels. They will occasionally grant this same glyph to their favoured champions, so that all who face them can witness their triumphs.

The striking crimson armour of the Novokh recalls the dynasty's violent history, and the bloody rituals they once observed. Come the battle's end, their silver frames have often turned a similar deep red – the colour of arterial gore.

# THOKT DYNASTY

The shifting void rifts of the Hyrakii Deeps hide the coreworlds of the Thokt Dynasty. These planets orbit the massive Meghoshta crownworld in a stately dance across the aeons, and smaller, heavily weaponised planetoids orbit them in turn. Wreathed in sparking blue energy, the crystalline continent-tombs of the Thokt Dynasty feed upon the radioactive power of the void rifts that surround them, the sky overhead thick with rippling darkness and flickering blue comets. As their armies emerge from their stasis-crypts to bring death to their foes, dull metal skulls reflect the cold sapphire stars far above.

Harnessing this potent radiation, the Thokt Crypteks have fashioned rad-receptors into the weaponry of their soldiers, a symptom of which is the shimmering azure light that emanates from their eyes, gauss flayers and even the cracks in their mechanical forms, debilitating and weakening those with bodies of flesh and blood. When the Thokt gather for war, the icy power of the Hyrakii void rifts becomes a truly baleful weapon.

The incomplete circles of the Thokt's dynastic symbol show the alignment of the Hyrakii Deeps to the crown and coreworlds of the dynasty's systems.

# CHARNOVOKH DYNASTY

Ravaged by the coming of the Tyranid hive fleets, the legions of Charnovokh cling defiantly to the edges of the Eastern Fringe. Their crypts have been overrun by the burrowing organisms of the Great Devourer, and many of their tomb worlds have been defiled by the Imperium, unwise settlers building high upon a foundation of slumbering dooms to come. Their dynasty is currently marshalling its remaining forces – only the strong have survived their misfortunes, however, and as Lords and Overlords put aside their petty differences, they are finding their mismatched legions are elite indeed.

In honour of their destroyed coreworlds, the Charnovokh bear the colours of Night Unending – jade energy signatures and dark-blue markings upon skull, shoulder and weapon. The higher a Necron's rank within the dynasty, the more of these colours he wears. Phaeron Thoekh's living-metal body is entirely midnight blue, his regal form swathed by a shroud of captive shadow that can teleport him from harm's way at the twitch of his finger.

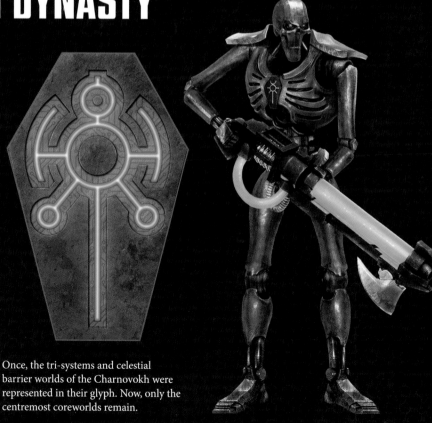

Once, the tri-systems and celestial barrier worlds of the Charnovokh were represented in their glyph. Now, only the centremost coreworlds remain.

# NEKTHYST DYNASTY

The Nekthyst are a dynasty of dented grandeur and stubborn pride. Long ago their ruler, the great conqueror Phaeron Oblis the Enslaver, angered the Triarch by refusing to adhere to their decrees. Thus, when the Nekthyst's crownworld of Moebius came under assault by a colossal Ork Waaagh!, the Triarch refused to rally to their subject's aid. Though the Orks were repelled, Moebius was devastated in the ensuing battle, along with much of the Nekthyst's once-glorious empire.

Ever since that day, the Nekthyst have shunned the concepts of honour and verity so prized by their kin, exchanging their traditional gold and purple heraldry for harsh, blackened copper carapaces that embody their jaded cynicism. They fight ruthlessly to preserve their shattered domain, using any and all methods – no matter how cruel or underhanded – to preserve their legacy. Though technically subjects of the greater empire, the Nekthyst are seen by the other Necron dynasties as little more than untrustworthy savages.

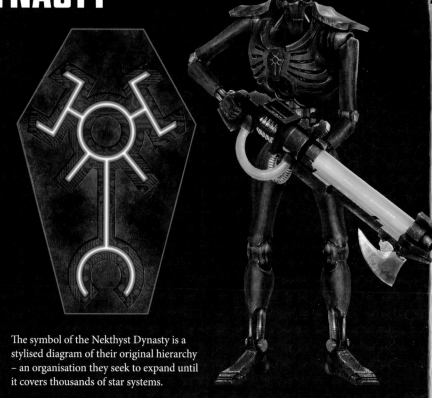

The symbol of the Nekthyst Dynasty is a stylised diagram of their original hierarchy – an organisation they seek to expand until it covers thousands of star systems.

# OGDOBEKH DYNASTY

Long ago the Ogdobekh came to an accord with the Crypteks who advised their ruling nobles. For millennia the two factions existed in a technological symbiosis, with the vast resources of the Ogdobekh coreworlds given over in exchange for the war machines and Canoptek constructs that allowed them to expand their realm ever further. Though they were at that point considered a minor power, their influence grew steadily with each passing decade. The phaeron of the Ogdobekh Dynasty, Anathrosis of the Black Star, was known for his paranoid streak – perhaps due to the rather superior behaviour of the Crypteks that formed a large part of his court. At all times he surrounded himself with an army of Canoptek constructs that could restore the glory of his legions should they be compromised. His tomb complexes were built with triple-layered backup systems, which proved to be of immense value over the course of the Great Sleep – when the dynasty awoke, the vehicles, constructs and warriors of the Ogdobekh emerged from their tombs all but intact. They have made impressive gains ever since.

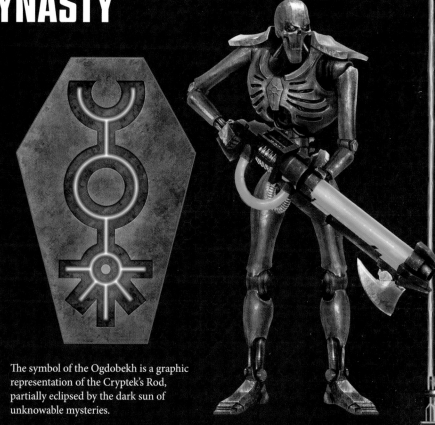

The symbol of the Ogdobekh is a graphic representation of the Cryptek's Rod, partially eclipsed by the dark sun of unknowable mysteries.

# A NEW EPOCH BEGINS

With every passing year, more and more Necron tomb worlds awaken from their millennia-long slumber, unleashing their legions upon a war-ravaged galaxy. Vast swathes of the ancient Necron Empire have already been reclaimed, and this relentless pace of expansion shows no sign of slowing.

## M41 AN ANCIENT THREAT RISES

### The Return of the Silent King

In c.744.M41, the Silent King enters the bounds of the galaxy once more. Having encountered the Tyranids in the intergalactic void, he realises that if these horrifying creatures are left unchecked they may consume every living thing in the galaxy before the Necrons can achieve their apotheosis. Returning from his self-imposed exile, the Silent King begins a pilgrimage across the galaxy, stirring tomb worlds yet to revive and speeding the recovery of those already awakened. Though he takes pains to conceal his true identity – working through Triarch Praetorians or unwitting Crypteks and Overlords – the Silent King's influence is felt from one side of the galaxy to the other. Slowly, he pursues his great work from the shadows, hoping that it is not already too late to atone for his past failures.

### The Rise of the Stormlord

After a decade of fruitless civil war, one of the many Overlords contesting the Mandragoran throne awakens Nemesor Imotekh to champion his cause. Appalled by the fruitless fighting that surrounds him, Imotekh gathers an army of his own and takes power for himself. Enforcing an iron rule and executing any noble foolish enough to stand in his path, Imotekh cements his position, naming himself phaeron of the Sautekh Dynasty. Within a year the dolmen gates of Mandragora are awakened, and Imotekh's reconquest of the galaxy begins in earnest.

### Death on Daxos

The addled yet brilliant Nemesor Zahndrekh eradicates the Ork hordes of Warboss Snagratoof on the tomb world of Daxos. This victory sees the last Ork infestations purged from the Sautekh coreworlds of old, while incidentally ending the decade-long war between Snagratoof's greenskins and the neighbouring Ecclesiarchal system of Haydn's Breach. The Haydnite Ecclesiarchy give thanks for this miracle from the Emperor, and the system thrives once more, never suspecting the true nature of their unwitting saviours.

### Bitter Vindication

The rise of Imotekh the Stormlord has come to pass, proving true the Prophecy of Doom Arising from the Book of Mournful Night. With this revelation, the Seer Councils of the craftworlds are forced to concede that the danger prophesied by the Alaitoc Aeldari is very real. There is no time for recrimination, however, for the threat is growing by the day and only the Aeldari understand its true scale. Once, a great crystalline map marked the locations of every tomb world in the galaxy – now, only fragments remain, and it is these that the Aeldari of Alaitoc use in conjunction with their far-flung networks of Exodites and Outcasts to begin to orchestrate the battle against the Necron menace. Even as other craftworlds are re-honing half-remembered strategies or debating the best course of action, the people of Alaitoc strike pre-emptively at slumbering tomb worlds and the legions of the risen.

### The Secrets of Solemnace

When the planet Solemnace is mysteriously bypassed by the life-scourging horrors of Hive Fleet Behemoth, the Inquisition takes an interest in precisely why. Inquisitor Valeria leads a force to investigate this anomaly, and discovers the myriad marvels of Solemnace's sprawling galleries, domain of the archaeovist Trazyn the Infinite. However, as the wide-eyed intruders make their way deeper into Solemnace's depths, the tomb world stirs to angry life around them. The running battle that ensues wreaks havoc and destruction through several of Trazyn's most prized exhibits, leading Solemnace's ruler to take

the field in person. As the fighting reaches a crescendo, Valeria herself guns down Trazyn with her graviton beamer, only to see the Lord of Solemnace stride from the shadows once more, hale and unharmed. The Inquisitorial force retreats, their few survivors falling back to their shuttles and leaving Solemnace to its secrets.

### Heralds of the Silent King

Since the return of the Silent King, the Triarch Praetorians have slowly become aware of his presence in the galaxy and have returned to his service one fragmented host at a time, officially restoring their oaths of fealty to their ancient liege. Many hundreds assemble on the tomb world of Antrakh to give their oaths in person, while thousands more join the gathering as hard-light holograms beamed from strongholds and tomb ships the galaxy over. The Praetorians swear to serve as the Silent King's heralds, keeping his identity a secret while spreading his message of unity to every tomb world they encounter. They will unify the Necron Empire in the face of the Tyranid threat, or face final, lasting death in the attempt.

### Thanatos Besieged

Heretic Astartes of the Word Bearers Legion descend in force upon the tomb world of Thanatos. Defended by the mighty legions of the Oruscar Dynasty, this world contains an incredible treasure – the Celestial Orrery. Were the zealot brethren of the Word Bearers to acquire the Orrery's power the consequences would be unthinkable. So begins a bloody, long-running siege, Necron Warriors and Immortals battling across the mountainous high-gravity surface of Thanatos against roaring Daemon Engines and fanatical Word Bearers. The conflict ends only when reinforcements from the Kardenath Dynasty arrive and crush the Word Bearers between their legions and those of the Oruscari. The war, however, does not finish there, for the Kardenath nobility are pursuing their own omnicidal campaign of destruction, and desire access to the Celestial Orrery to see it completed. When Oruscar's Phaeron Hakmephet refuses, Thanatos is reduced to a battleground once again, this time seeing Necron pitted against Necron in a grinding siege that shows no signs of ending.

### The Ruin of Morrigar
A battle between hive gangs on Morrigar inadvertently awakens the Necron tomb hidden there. All contact with Morrigar is lost shortly thereafter. When the Cadian 207th makes planetfall six months later, there is no trace of any inhabitants, human or otherwise. Before the Astra Militarum can leave Morrigar, the nomadic Necron warlord, Anrakyr the Traveller, arrives. Assuming the humans are responsible for the apparent destruction of the tomb world, he launches an attack that leaves his own forces decimated and the Cadian 207th utterly eliminated.

### The Disappearance of Explorator Fleet 913
Explorator Fleet 913 strays into territory controlled by the Nihilakh crownworld of Gheden and is destroyed by the fleet of Nemesor Azderon. When the battle is done, wreckage is set adrift in the projected trajectory of Craftworld Alaitoc. By the time three companies of Ultramarines come in search of the explorator fleet, Azderon has long withdrawn, but the presence of Alaitoc's pathfinder vessels draw the Space Marines into conflict with the Aeldari.

### The Triumphant Return of Thaszar the Invincible
The shadow-shrouded world of Athonos is wracked by severe earth tremors. The cause remains a mystery until a colossal tomb ship captained by the Pirate King, Thaszar the Invincible, emerges from beneath the ground, shedding soil, rock and fragments of hab-block from its hull as it rises. The world's defences are, understandably, in disarray. Fortunately for the inhabitants, Thaszar has yet to realise that humans are an intelligent form of life, and pays no more attention to the panicked defenders than he would to a nest of insects. The Athonosian planetary capital lies in ruins, but the rest of the planet survives relatively unscathed as the tomb ship heads into the stars towards the tomb world of Zapennec, pausing only to obliterate a holo-stealthed Aeldari listening post hidden in near orbit. Upon reaching the tomb world, Thaszar manipulates the master program into believing him the planet's rightful phaeron. Seizing control of the world and all its awakened warriors, Thaszar restyles Zapennec as the Reaveworld, transforming it into a mighty pirate stronghold. His

underlings gather ships from the large belt of orbital wreckage left by the last great space battle of the War in Heaven, and the raiding begins in earnest.

## M41 THE DYNASTIES REVEALED
### Sanctuary 101
The armies of the Sautekh Dynasty continue their relentless advance across the Vidar Sector, sweeping into Imperial space at last. Imotekh the Stormlord leads an attack against the fortress convent on Sanctuary 101. The Sisters of Battle within fight like lions, doing all they can to preserve a lasting record of this previously unknown threat. They are raised in the Emperor's sight as a result, living on in the legends of their order. Yet for all their defiance they are slain, their pict-captures revealing little more than blurred and stalking shadows.

### Fear Has A Name
Following recovery of the footage from Sanctuary 101, a number of Ordo Xenos Inquisitors come to a chilling realisation. Pooling intelligence from dozens of filed, pending or redacted reports – some of which must be reclaimed from the Administratum at gunpoint – they realise this mysterious xenos threat is at large throughout the galaxy. Presenting their findings to the High Lords in person, the Inquisitors succeed in having these half-glimpsed Necrons recognised as a vermilion-class threat. However, between the secretive nature of the Inquisitorial Ordos, the ponderous bureaucracy of the Administratum and the terrible difficulties of interstellar communication, it will be many years before the Imperium at large is properly warned of this new foe.

### The Kingdom of Bone
A strike force of Dark Angels bypasses the blockade of the Ghoul Stars, plunging into this haunted realm of space in pursuit of a battle-brother they believe to be one of the

Fallen. The grim-faced Space Marines run their quarry to ground on a charnel planet of ash and bone, only to discover that they have been pursuing the animate cadaver of a loyal 4th Company Sergeant. As the corpse flops to the ground with metallic mindshackle scarabs pouring from its eyes and mouth, the wastes come alive with shrieking, hissing packs of Flayed Ones. The Dark Angels have been lured into the Bone Kingdom of Drazak by its mad king Valgul, there to sate the hunger of his twisted kin.

The Space Marines fall into a tight defensive formation, fighting back-to-back as the shrieking tide of blade-fingered automata crashes down upon them. Blood flows, bolters roar and the charnel plains ring to the sound of blades clashing against steely talons. For over an hour the Flayed Ones fight frantically to overwhelm their outnumbered prey. The Dark Angels are only saved when their Strike Cruiser, *Lion's Roar*, performs a near-suicidal attack run through the upper atmosphere, fighting the planet's gravity just long enough to drive the Necrons back with massed bombardments and teleport the surviving battle-brothers to safety. With their quarry fled, the Flayed Ones feast, the crash of battle replaced by an obscene chorus of crunching, cracking and tearing that goes on for many hours into the night.

### Mass Abductions
The Imperial world of Mandal begins to experience frequent night-time raids by wings of Night Scythes. Entire farming communities are snatched up in the dark, whole townships disappearing without trace. Unbeknownst to the planet's defenders, the source of the trouble is the small moon of Trantis, a Necron way-station that has awoken and – following ancient directives – begun to stockpile Mandal's resources for redistribution to other worlds. Ironically, Trantis' dolmen gate has long been severed from the webway, leaving the moon drowning in accumulated wealth for which it has no use. Yet still the raids continue…

### A War Without Honour
The legions of the Nekthyst Dynasty attack a trio of Imperial factory worlds known as the Threefold Engels. Deploying teams of Deathmarks and swarms of Canoptek Wraiths, they mislead the command structure of the Astra Militarum forces into defending a string of far-flung islands whilst a concerted attack falls upon

the mainland. Engel Prime and Engel Secundus fall in a matter of weeks, their defenders fighting valiantly but without cohesion against the duplicitous foe. Only on Engel Tertius does Nekthyst Nemesor Suthtis encounter stiff resistance, for here an embedded regiment of Cadian Baneblades turn the tide with their sheer armoured might. In response, Suthtis unleashes no less than three separate shards of the C'tan known as the Deceiver. The godling's illusions and trickery throw the foe into utter confusion, allowing Nekthyst forces to close in on and destroy the Baneblades, ending the Cadian resistance at a stroke. The Nekthyst Dynasty claims the Threefold Engels as their own, renaming them the Shadowed Triad and awakening the tomb hidden deep beneath Engel Secundus.

### The Fall of Hypnoth

Imotekh's campaigns are halted briefly by the Imperium's resolute defence of forge world Hypnoth. Astra Militarum and Space Marine reinforcements flood into the battle zone, and though they cannot achieve a lasting victory, they succeed in tying down the Necron assault for several months. Encouraged by the prophecies of the astromancer Orikan the Diviner, Imotekh finally breaks the stalemate by launching a series of attacks on Hypnoth's supply worlds, Praedis-Zeta and Nyx. The first two raids perform entirely as expected, with the planets laid waste and their vital supplies claimed by the Sautekh forces. However, an unforeseen Tyranid infestation on Nyx wreaks havoc amongst the Necron forces and threatens to derail Imotekh's entire campaign. The Stormlord weaves a strategy that manipulates the Tyranid swarm into attacking the remaining Imperial defenders, allowing Imotekh to extricate his remaining forces and continue on his campaign. Meanwhile, Sautekh Crypteks succeed in introducing a mechanophage into the defence systems of Hypnoth, reducing its formidably armed bastions to helpless ferrocrete shells. Despite a valorous defence by Space Marines of the Flesh Tearers and Iron Hands Chapters, Hypnoth is conquered.

### The Twisted Catacombs

In retaliation for the attack upon the Threefold Engels, the Ordo Xenos dispatches a Deathwatch Kill Team to destroy Moebius, the crownworld of the Nekthyst Dynasty. So tangled is the maze of hyperspace corridors that make up this shadowed world, the Deathwatch

battle-brothers are soon divided and hopelessly lost. Only one brother escapes alive, a Space Wolf by the name of Ranulf Longstriker, but he has been rendered hopelessly insane by his experiences.

### The Sands of Fordris

Warboss Skullkrak leads a mob of his best boyz to the ghost world of Fordris, chasing rumours of ancient and deadly weaponry. However, his expedition meets a messy end upon a nameless beach as wave upon wave of Necrons march from the blood-red waters of the ocean. The Orks are wiped out to the last, but not before Fordris' Crypteks have gathered reams of useful combat data. However, the Mephrit masters of Fordris judge their warriors to be at only seventy per cent combat efficiency. Seeking more data, they lure an arcanological expedition of the Adeptus Mechanicus to their world. It is not long before the sands are stained red once more.

### Broken Faith

Anrakyr the Traveller attacks the Imperial shrine world of Saintspyre. So stout are this world's defences and so easily has it seen off previous invaders that it is believed throughout the system that the Emperor himself protects it. The Traveller will prove this claim false. Anrakyr's Crypteks have confirmed that the tomb complex at the shrine world's heart is cold and dead, plundered many centuries ago by the ignorant human settlers. Accordingly, the Traveller is here to exact a terrible revenge. Using his tomb ships as a shield to ward off the planet's fleet, Anrakyr fights his way through to the greatest of Saintspyre's orbital fortresses, the *Blade Imperium*. Waves of Night Scythes scream around the fortress' sprawling hull, beaming rank upon rank of attackers onto its armoured

hide. Impervious to the dangers of hard vacuum, Anrakyr's Pyrrhian Eternals blast their way into the *Blade Imperium*, venting the fortress' atmosphere at a dozen key points. Hundreds of luckless humans are flung screaming into the void, Necron Immortals striding dispassionately down corridors splattered with the frozen remains of decompressed Imperial troopers. As Anrakyr himself makes his way into the fortress, the surviving garrison stage a final fight back, but in a bloody, one-sided gun battle across the Primus Concordium, the Necrons make short work of their assailants. Anrakyr now strikes the killing blow, channelling his furious will into the mighty weapon systems of the *Blade Imperium* and discharging its cyclopean batteries at the planet below. The bombardment is so horrifically destructive that it shatters the planet's crust and breaches its core, condemning Saintspyre to a slow and fiery death.

As Anrakyr departs the doomed world, morale throughout the system collapses, beginning a chain reaction that will sweep an entire segmentum with panic. After this day, Necron attacks will hold a new terror for the people of the Imperium, for if even the shield of the Emperor cannot hold this foe at bay, what chance does Humanity stand?

## M41 THE GALAXY BESIEGED

### The War of Uttu Prime

After his foes refuse his generous terms of surrender, Nemesor Zahndrekh launches a devastating attack upon the planet of Uttu Prime. He is opposed by regiments of Catachans and no fewer than three companies of Imperial Fists, yet the power of his legions cannot be denied. Though they fight with the courage of heroes, the Imperial forces suffer horrific casualties when Zahndrekh unleashes an ancient war engine known as the Megalith. The last Imperial defenders stage a brave stand in the governor's citadel, dying one by one in a close and bloody battle with Vargard Obyron and Zahndrekh's Lychguard.

### The Rise of Damnos

After incautious mining operations disturb their slumber, the Necrons under the icy crust of Damnos wake swiftly to full function. They overwhelm the human settlers and repel a counter-attack by the Ultramarines 2nd Company. The Necrons of Damnos then proceed to awaken their dolmen gates and reconquer a crucial spar of the webway, driving out the Aeldari who had reclaimed its paths during the Great Sleep. With their webway access restored, raiding parties from Damnos reach out across the Ultima Segmentum, leaving carnage in their wake. The blow to Imperial morale is severe – for the twenty-five years that follow, Cato Sicarius is so haunted by his failure he does not smile even once.

### The Beast Slain
The T'au sept world of Uan'voss is almost overrun by a sudden onslaught of Tyranids, only to be rescued by the most unlikely of saviours. Several legions of Necrons from the Atun Dynasty fall upon the swarming bio-horrors, their Monoliths and Annihilation Barges laying down a crippling bombardment of fire while a spearhead of Triarch Praetorians cut their way deep into the monstrous horde. Though the swarm fights back with the fury of a wounded beast, the Tyranids are caught between the attacking Necrons and the firepower of the surviving T'au. As the last chitinous horrors crash down dead, the entire Necron army turns on its collective heel and departs without a word of explanation. The bewildered T'au can do little but give thanks for their mysterious rescue, little knowing they have just witnessed the servants of the Silent King.

### Conqueror's Fall
Whilst en route to the Sautekh coreworld of Davatas, the Stormlord's tomb ship *Inevitable Conqueror* comes under attack by a Black Templars fleet. Leading the assault is none other than High Marshal Helbrecht, come searching for a long anticipated revenge upon the warlord who humbled him and cut off his right hand upon Schrödinger VII. A broadside from the Battle Barge *Sigismund* strips away the Necron ship's shields an instant before the Black Templars' boarding torpedoes strike home and, within moments, the decks of the *Inevitable Conqueror* are prowled by vengeful Space Marines. Pride compels Imotekh to stand and fight, but his forces are in disarray and logic wins out. The Stormlord teleports to an escort vessel and makes his escape. Helbrecht is incandescent with fury, but consoles himself by personally setting Imotekh's beloved flagship on a collision course with a nearby star, and annihilating those other Necron craft too slow to flee. It is a crushing blow to the Stormlord's pride, and one that will not be soon forgotten.

### An Unforgivable Theft
Illuminor Szeras leads warriors of the Sautekh Dynasty in an attack upon the Imperial world of Gorszt, destroying a fortress complex belonging to the Mentors Space Marine Chapter. As his prize, Szeras claims the entire stock of precious gene-seed that lies hidden beneath the fortress.

### Vengeance at Damnos
Twenty-five years after the Necrons drove the Imperium from Damnos, Marneus Calgar returns at the head of a massive force of Ultramarines, Astra Militarum and Deathwatch Kill Teams. The Damnosian nobility defend their world with everything they have, viewing this invasion with a mixture of contempt and outrage. The Space Marines and their allies sustain punishing casualties, whereas the Necrons rise from the blood-stained snows time and time again. As the battle reaches its height the Necrons unleash the might of their Baleful Necropolis. This airborne tomb complex dominates the fight – mighty blasts of entropic energy from its Monoliths and the Tesseract Vault at its heart lash the Space Marine lines while the ground beneath them yawns into gnashing chasms. Only the desperate actions of Marneus Calgar himself see the Necropolis destroyed and the Transcendent C'tan set loose from its cage. Utter carnage follows, for the wrath of the vengeful star god is unleashed upon both armies. Captain Cato Sicarius saves the battered remnants of the Imperial force with a well-timed vortex grenade that obliterates the C'tan entirely. Damnos' Necrons are laid low, their leaders slain and their resurrection made impossible through the destruction of their stasis-crypts.

### The Great Rift
The Black Crusades of Abaddon the Despoiler culminate in a disaster of cosmic magnitude. Unbeknownst to the Imperium – and even to the Necrons – the Warmaster of Chaos has enacted a ten-thousand-year mission of demolition upon the structures the ancient Necrontyr raised to keep the warp from spilling into realspace. The Citadel of the Kromarch, the pylons of Cadia and a dozen other astromantic locations are torn down, leaving wounds in reality that reach critical mass and join together to form the Cicatrix Maledictum.

### The Absorption Wars
Imotekh the Stormlord launches a series of extensive reconquests, intending to absorb those tomb worlds awakened by the Great Rift into the Sautekh Dynasty. The Necrons clash with the daemonic menace on a dozen different worlds, with a will to cleanse the newly aware planets and hence put their dynasties in his debt. With one side epitomising cold logic and order, and the other the white heat of chaos, neither can predict or understand their opponent. Casualties on both sides spiral into the billions, but Imotekh does not relent.

### Foundation of Sand
On the orders of Belisarius Cawl, Magos Dominus Dentrex Ologostion leads an excavation party to unearth the blackstone buried beneath the surface of the forge world Amontep II. No sooner has an array of noctilith obelisks been uncovered than rank after rank of Necrons arises from the rust-coloured sand. The ensuing battle-data that pours into Ologostion's tactical partition reveals an inescapable truth – the ancient forge world of Amotep II is home to an even more ancient presence, one that has remained hidden from the Adeptus Mechanicus' most invasive geoscopic surveys for millennia.

### The Legions Awoken
By this point, even the most hopeful estimates of the Imperium suggest that more than a thousand tomb worlds have awoken, though the Aeldari know the number to be greater still. Between the efforts of the Triarch Praetorians, Anrakyr the Traveller, Imotekh the Stormlord and the many dozens of lesser phaerons and nemesors scattered across the galaxy, the Necron race is waking with ever-increasing speed. Billions of Necrons still slumber, yet legion upon legion now bestride the stars. Every day their ranks grow in number, and as they march forward the galaxy trembles.

The Ultramarines and the Necrons of the Sautekh Dynasty have a fierce rivalry, stemming from the apocalyptic battles for the tomb world of Damnos. Imotekh the Stormlord has sworn to see the Space Marine Chapter utterly destroyed, their home world burned to ash, and their commanders dragged before him in chains, so that they may know the true cost of their defiance.

# IMOTEKH THE STORMLORD

## PHAERON OF THE SAUTEKH DYNASTY

Nemesor Imotekh awoke from the Great Sleep to find his tomb world in disarray. Mandragora had survived the aeons mostly intact, only to fall foul of unrestrained ambition. The crownworld's phaeron had been one of the few to perish during hibernation and, once they had quashed immediate alien threats, the remaining nobles had moved to seize the throne. A decade of internecine civil war followed, with no faction able to gain victory. During this time, the revivification of high-ranking nobles was suspended, as neither side wished to awaken further competitors. Had the situation continued, Imotekh would likely have slumbered until the civil war had torn Mandragora apart. As it was, one of the pretenders struck upon the idea of recruiting the famous general to his cause – with such a supporter in thrall, victory could not fail to be his.

However, when Imotekh awoke, he was both enraged and appalled at the anarchy about him. Realising that Mandragora's only hope of restoration lay in the civil war ending as swiftly as possible, he refused to support either faction. Instead, Imotekh marshalled an army of his own, destroyed the chief antagonists, and claimed Mandragora's throne for himself. The newly crowned phaeron thereafter forbade any form of infighting within his realm, declaring such activities to be a waste of time, effort and resource. This law was ill-observed at first, but swiftly became the norm once Imotekh had proven his willingness to make terminal examples of those who flouted his authority. Between this rule of iron and a swift string of military successes against nearby worlds, Imotekh's position soon became unassailable. Indeed, to this day his only true rival is the famed Nemesor Zahndrekh of the crownworld of Gidrim, but the old general's loyalty is as unquestionable as his wits are addled, so he is of little threat.

Imotekh is a grand strategist, perhaps the most accomplished the galaxy has ever known. His campaigns operate not only across worlds, but across entire star systems and sectors. When Imotekh launches an attack, it is impossible to discern if it is the main thrust of his strategy or simply a decoy raid, crafted to bleed enemy reinforcements away from a battle yet to come. All such assaults are carefully weighted to overwhelm forces already in place, requiring the foe to either sacrifice their troops or reinforce them – and Imotekh's plans are always many stages ahead, set to take advantage of either course. Indeed, the Stormlord's battle plans are incredibly versatile, seeded with feint attacks, counter-strategies and other contingencies enacted automatically should certain circumstances be triggered or thresholds crossed. To outside observers there is something almost mystical to Imotekh's methodology, for how else could he so flawlessly anticipate the unseen? Yet in truth there is nothing more at play here than the careful application of probabilities and logic, combined with a canny understanding of the foe's mindset.

So impeccable are the logical patterns behind the Stormlord's strategies that the only way a foe can truly gain meaningful advantage is to abandon all logic themselves – something that most enemies find incredibly difficult to do, but Orkish anarchy achieves as naturally as breathing. Thus does the Stormlord hate Orks above all the lesser races of the galaxy for, no matter how hard he tries, he rarely wins a lasting victory over the rabblesome greenskins. Yet lasting victories against the Orks there must be, for Imotekh's goal is nothing less than to wipe them from the face of the galaxy. The Stormlord is unshakeable in his belief that only when the galaxy is washed clean with the blood of inferior beings will Necron dominance begin anew.

As phaeron of the Sautekh, Imotekh can draw upon incredible resources, for the armies of the entire dynasty are his to requisition at need. Yet the Stormlord knows that the foe – all other sentient life – is too numerous for victory to be won through force of arms alone. Thus, for Imotekh, terror is a weapon as potent

as any in the Necron arsenal, and one he employs to full effect. His armies advance under the cover of storm-blackened skies, emerald lightning bolts arcing out from heavy clouds to wreak carnage amongst the foe. Enemy armies that advance into the shadow of the storm are simply swallowed up, cut off from all contact whilst the battle lasts. Any warriors that escape from the maelstrom's clutches do so only to sow panic, fear and dismay amongst their comrades. Worse, some such survivors are implanted with bloodswarm nanoscarabs, whose gore-warm scent acts as an irresistible beacon for roaming packs of Flayed Ones.

If the Stormlord has one weakness, it is a prideful need to display his superiority over those enemy commanders foolish enough to stand against him. High-ranking enemies are often set free upon their defeat so that they will have to live with the knowledge of their inadequacy. This is a lesson invariably reinforced by physical mutilation – a severed limb normally being the favoured method. Yet with every battle, these surviving foes learn a little more of the Stormlord's methods and the best of them only become more determined to see his campaigns ended once and for all. High Marshal Helbrecht of the Black Templars, in particular, has run the Stormlord close on more than one occasion, though victory has thus far escaped his grasp.

The fact that Imotekh suffers from such a personal form of martial hubris stands in stark contrast to the analytical and emotionless detachment he displays when planning and conducting campaigns. It is possible that stasis-induced eccentricity is to blame, but for which trait? Is Imotekh a master strategist whose engrammic

damage spurs him to seek personal glory, or a bellicose warrior granted strategic genius through an accident of fate? In the end, it does not matter. If Imotekh's defeat comes, it is sure not to be at the hands of a superior strategist, but rather at the hands of a more accomplished warrior.

And there will be many opportunities for such a downfall. Imotekh's domain is growing at a rate unparalleled amongst the Necron dynasties. Over a hundred tomb worlds lie under his regal command, and five times as many alien-held planets pay direct or indirect tribute – the number of alien civilisations Imotekh has destroyed during his campaigns cannot easily be counted. Such a realm is as nothing when compared to the galaxy-spanning Imperium or the Necron dynasties at the height of their glory, but is nonetheless impressive for the work of mere centuries.

The rapid expansion of Imotekh's dynasty has now come crashing violently into the domains of other star-spanning empires. On Macragge, reports of Necron activity along Ultramar's northern borders have reached the attention of Marneus Calgar. Craftworld Iyanden also faces danger from the Sautekh legions, as great a threat as the continued Tyranid menace and the daemonic invasions that are now pouring from the Great Rift. The long advance upon the T'au Empire has also come to destructive fruition, with Imotekh's invasion fleets tearing into the territories of the young race. As new systems are subsumed by the Sautekh Dynasty, so too are more tomb worlds brought into Imotekh's fold, growing his armies as more slumbering warriors are awakened. Yet these are only the earliest rumblings of the Stormlord's tempest.

## MANDRAGORA THE GOLDEN

Mandragora was always an important world, a hub for the Necron armies that did battle on the eastern rim of the galaxy. It was built as a shining, gilded world of glorious mausoleums and towering sepulchres, the physical manifestation of the Necrontyr obsession with death.

When the War in Heaven ended, Mandragora's stasis-crypts were filled with some of the finest warriors of the Necron dynasties. The planet's defences were second to none, as befitted a world of its status, and it survived the Great Sleep intact. So did Mandragora emerge from hibernation with vast legions at its disposal – a situation its new phaeron, Imotekh, was quick to exploit by immediately launching a campaign to conquer dozens of nearby coreworlds.

# OVERLORDS & LORDS

One of the great marvels of Necron engineering is the resurrection orb, a glowing sphere of precious metals that possesses the ability to overcharge the regenerative capabilities of nearby Necrons. When activated, this device unleashes an intense burst of radiation which revitalises and reactivates the self-repair routines of even the most badly damaged warrior of the dynasties. With eerie synchronicity, the shattered and broken forms of slain Necrons begin to shift and crawl back together, their living-metal skeletons reforming with terrifying speed. These relics are incredibly rare and valuable, and are granted only to the highest-ranking Lords and Overlords of the empire.

As befitted their rank, the nobles of the Necron kingdoms emerged far better from biotransference than did the plebeian classes. Not only were their new bodies stronger and more durable, but the engrammic circuitry that housed each noble's intellect and personality was far more extensive than that granted to lesser Necrontyr. Most Necrons emerge from the Great Sleep as dull-witted creatures, with little memory of the individual they once were. By contrast, unless they suffer damage during their dormancy, Necron Lords and Overlords retain all the drives, obsessions and nuances of personality that they once possessed.

A tomb world may have dozens, or even hundreds, of nobles, but only one has the power of absolute rule. For coreworlds and fringeworlds this is usually a Lord, while crownworlds and particularly important coreworlds will have Overlords as their regents. Each phaeron will also lay claim to a crownworld, from which he rules his entire dynasty. Amongst a tomb world's nobles, political infighting is rife and there are always insidious schemes playing out, albeit at an interminable pace. As a result of their android nature, Necrons tend towards calculative behaviour, and a pretender will rarely move openly if the chances of success are outweighed by the probability of failure.

Yet if the prize is large enough, internal power struggles can erupt into open conflict. When this occurs, the remainder of the tomb world's nobles align according to allegiance and ambition, though some will wait as long as possible before doing so whilst they negotiate the price of their loyalty. These internal wars invariably follow the formalised codes that governed the ancient Necrontyr, leading to battles with forces arranged and rules agreed in advance by the competitors. In times before biotransference, such events led to the slaughter of countless millions. Nowadays, thanks to the Necrons' capacity for self-repair, these wars can last for years or even centuries with no discernible victor.

For every battle a Necron noble fights amongst his own kind, he will orchestrate hundreds of sprawling campaigns against alien usurpers who squat amongst the remains of the Necron dynasties. For many nemesors, it is unthinkable to honour an alien enemy with the traditional codes of battle. In their eyes, most races are little more than vermin to be wiped away with as much efficiency and as little pomp as possible. Many of the more advanced races, such as the Aeldari, have simply proven themselves unworthy of being treated as equals. So it is that assassination and ambush – forms of battle forbidden in wars between the nobility – are employed against outsiders without reservation. Yet no matter how base a Necron ruler might consider his enemy to be, he will personally lead his vassals from the thick of the fighting whenever possible. Thus does he prove his superiority.

When a Necron Lord or Overlord strides forth in his raiment of war, only the strongest and canniest of enemies have any hope of survival. His armoured form is proof against tank-busting weaponry; his metal sinews have might enough to crush bones to powder. At his command are all the arcane armaments of his ancient civilisation: warscythes, staffs of light and other wondrous tools of destruction. Yet perhaps a Necron noble's most potent weapon is his mind. Indeed, a phaeron has so much force of will that he can infuse nearby minions with a portion of his own burning determination, creating an unstoppable core of resistance against any foe.

# CATACOMB COMMAND BARGES

The more aggressive Necron Overlords fight not on foot, but rather from the deck of a Catacomb Command Barge – an armoured, repulsor-driven skimmer. In ancient times, this craft would hover high above the army, so that all Necrontyr could see their Overlord's presence and take heart from it. Most Overlords can no longer directly inspire the soldiery as once they could – few Necrons any longer have the capacity to process such emotions – but technology has filled the void. The Catacomb Command Barge is nothing less than a giant carrier-wave generator that allows an Overlord to instantaneously issue commands to nearby troops. Even now, when inspiration has little to do with visibility, an Overlord will often seek a raised vantage point at battle's start, so he might better divine the enemy's intended strategy before it unfolds.

The Catacomb Command Barge itself is a swift and manoeuvrable craft – it has to be, for an Overlord must keep pace with the conflict at all times. Though the Overlord is undeniably the Command Barge's master,

he does not operate its controls. Such work is beneath nobility, and especially below those of such esteemed rank as his own. The craft's controls are the charge of the two slaved Necron crew, who act both as its pilots and as the gunners for its underslung weaponry. These Necrons are hard-wired to the Overlord through the craft and can react to his instructions in a fraction of a second. This does not, however, prevent the Overlord from issuing verbal commands – old habits die hard in old soldiers. Indeed, it is often possible to hear the Overlord's authoritative instructions or angry epithets echoing across a battlefield as he drives his crew hard up to, and sometimes beyond, their limits. Service aboard a Command Barge is considered to be a great honour, though it is not without its risks. Not only does it guarantee a place in the very heart of battle, but if the Overlord is slain – or sometimes even if he is merely put to inconvenience through mechanical failure – retribution falls upon his pilots.

With his barge's systems attended to by his minions, the Overlord is free to wield his

own weapons against the foe. Sometimes he will stand proud on the prow of his vehicle, swinging his blade at close quarters into the ranks of his enemies. At others, however, the Overlord will remain seated in his throne, choosing instead to unleash crackling blasts of energy as the Catacomb Command Barge screams past. The last sight of many an enemy has been that of a Catacomb Command Barge swooping out of the sky, the Overlord's energy-bladed weapon gleaming as it swings around in a decapitating arc…

# CRYPTEKS

Crypteks are members of pan-galactic conclaves of technologists whose purpose is to study and maintain the eldritch devices of their race. They are masters of dimensional dissonance, singularity manipulation, atomic transmutation, elemental transmogrification and countless other reason-defying technologies. In many ways, a Cryptek's powers mirror those employed by the psykers of other races, but with a crucial difference: instead of using a mutant mind to channel warp energies, the Cryptek employs arcane science to harness the universe's fundamental forces.

Every conclave specialises in a particular field of techno-sorcery, be it psychomancy, plasmancy, chronomancy or any one of a hundred thousand other disciplines. The conclaves were originally founded to share information and expertise from one end of the galaxy to the other, but have since become fragmented and isolated. In the millennia since biotransference, Crypteks have become just as stagnant and fragmented as every other aspect of Necron society. Nowadays, the surviving conclaves are maintained out of force of habit more than for any practical reason.

Though Crypteks have no official rank in the political structure of a dynasty, they wield incredible influence. The Necrontyr nobility was disinterested by the workings of the technology it employed, and this attitude has faded little with time. A Cryptek's power springs from this ignorance, and from the army of Canoptek Spyders, Wraiths and Scarabs under his control. Though few Necron nobles pay the idea much heed, a tomb world's countless systems require perpetual maintenance if they are to function at peak efficiency, and a slighted Cryptek is always willing to bring the cycle to a screaming halt should his 'betters' require a reminder. Even the proudest Overlord will muster an apology when his soldiers and weapons seize up.

On occasion, a Necron Overlord will go so far as to recruit an especially trusted and knowledgeable Cryptek to serve in his Royal Court, particularly in the case of the Ogdobekh Dynasty, where the Crypteks are possessed of a rare genius. Such a move can prove politically dangerous for the Overlord, as this essentially elevates the Cryptek to the same rank as the Necron Lords already serving there,

and so fosters resentment. Nonetheless, having the Cryptek's wealth of knowledge and expertise close at hand is more than adequate compensation.

Ultimately, the only thing that holds the ambitions of a Cryptek in check is another of his kind. Should a retained Cryptek rise too far above his station, a Necron Overlord will attempt to replace him by luring a more tractable Cryptek away from the service of a rival. Even this has complications, for whilst no Cryptek will knowingly supplant another of the same conclave, a rival from another conclave will happily do so.

Once his services are acquired, a Cryptek's duties stretch far beyond the tomb world. It is common for an Overlord to grant a Cryptek the first pickings of precious alloys, power cores and focus crystals in exchange for his services on campaign. Such a bargain serves both sides well; a tomb world's resources are limited, and the Cryptek's trade requires that he have a ready supply of raw materials.

For his part, the Overlord gains the full fury of the Cryptek's incredible techno-sorceries. With a mere gesture of his staff of light, a Cryptek can unleash bolts of searing viridian energy that melt through the thickest armour with ease. The chronometron is another favoured treasure amongst the Crypteks. This eye-shaped device can alter and shift the flow of time around its bearer, slowing incoming energy blasts and flying bullets to a crawl. To better observe the effects of their rampaging creations, some Crypteks utilise Canoptek cloaks to soar above the fray – each of these techno-arcane shrouds is attached to a spider-like construct that generates a powerful anti-gravity pressor field, allowing its wearer to speed through the air. This item also has a remarkable secondary function, able to stitch together a damaged necrodermis with its supple limbs and focused radiation beamers.

The technological marvels wielded by the Crypteks are the weapons of the gods, and only gods would think to stand against them.

# ILLUMINOR SZERAS
## ARCHITECT OF BIOTRANSFERENCE

The C'tan might have provided the knowledge for biotransference, but it was Szeras who made it a reality. Even then, he saw it as the first of several steps on the path to ultimate evolution, a journey that would end as a creature not of flesh or metal, but as a god of pure energy. Until that day, Szeras is driven to take full advantage of his android form. After all, no longer must he sleep nor deal with the thousand frailties and distractions to which flesh is heir.

Szeras labours to unravel the mysteries of life, for he fears that he would be a poor sort of god without such secrets at his fingertips. Szeras has been on the brink of understanding for many centuries, yet somehow final comprehension always escapes him. Perhaps there are some concepts in the universe that do not reveal themselves before logic, or perhaps it is simply that to understand life, the observer must stand amongst the ranks of the living, and not the undead. Whatever the reason, the truth is that the secrets of the soul will almost certainly lie forever beyond Szeras' comprehension. This is a truth that he will never accept. Yet, at times, Szeras must turn aside from his work and act in the interest of others – he requires a constant flow of living subjects, and the most efficient way for him to acquire such creatures is to trade expertise in exchange for captives.

Though Szeras is obsessed with the secrets of life, his aptitude for augmenting the weaponry and even the mechanical bodies of his fellow Necrons is peerless. Szeras' delving into the form and function of so many disparate living creatures has taught him how to augment almost every facet of Necron machinery – a trait seen as distasteful by many of his peers. The dissection of Vuzsalen Arachtoid compound eyes unlocked an improved array for targeting optics, and the molecular dissembling of chitinous Ambull hide led the way to more efficient armour configurations, to name but two of many thousands of such advances.

On occasion, Szeras' talents are in such demand that he can name his own price – invariably a harvesting raid targeted against a world of his choosing. Above all, Szeras cherishes Aeldari subjects, as they inevitably produce more intriguing results than any other of the galaxy's creatures. However, few Necron Overlords will deliberately transgress on Aeldari territory for reasons other than solid military gain, so Szeras finds such specimens the hardest of all to acquire. Szeras inevitably accompanies the initial waves of such an attack, the better to pick and choose the subjects that will make up his payment and ensure he is not cheated by his client.

Once seized, Szeras' specimens can look forward only to a pain-filled, though not necessarily brief, existence in the bloodstained and shadowed laboratory catacombs of Zantragora. Few of Szeras' operations are carried out on the dead, for he believes the knowledge he seeks resides only in the living. Banks of stasis machinery keep the subject alive and aware throughout the procedures, though they do nothing to numb the terrible pain. The specimens' agonised screams are of no consequence to Szeras, as he feels no kinship with such inferior beings. He simply shuts off his audio receptors until the repulsive noise subsides, watching impassively as his whirring tools carve the subject apart molecule by molecule.

# ORIKAN THE DIVINER

## SEER OF THE NECRONTYR

Orikan is a consummate astromancer, able to calculate the events of the future from the patterns of the stars. Thus did he know of the Fall of the Aeldari, the Rise of Man, the Horus Heresy, the coming of the Tyranids and the Great Rift many thousands of years before they came to pass. Through careful study and scrutiny, Orikan can even divine lesser occurrences: the movement of fleets, the destinies of individuals, even the strategies undertaken by campaigning armies – events not important enough to reshape the galaxy, but the foreknowledge of which can dramatically change the fortunes of the beholder.

Though they make use of his laborious studies, few amongst Orikan's peers truly trust him. This is not altogether to do with his skills, for all Crypteks are capable of techno-sorceries that defy belief. The unease that Orikan provokes is due chiefly to the mocking scorn with which he treats the nobility of every rank, and to the knowing gleam in his eye that implies he is party to a joke that no other can perceive. Many an Overlord would dearly like to see Orikan punished for this quiet insolence. However, not only is such a course of action impolitic – the benefits of being able to call upon Orikan's skills greatly outweigh any offence caused by his manner – it is also almost entirely impossible. Orikan knows the plans of his rivals and enemies long before they do, and it is child's play for him to exploit such schemes to his personal advantage – an alteration that, more often than not, involves a fatal outcome for the original plotter.

Skilled astromancer though he is, Orikan's predictions are not flawless. Unforeseen events can queer his calculations, altering, wiping out and replacing his prophesied timeline. Warp travel is a consistent aggravation, as its eddies and anarchies seem to delight in defying his predictions. Under such circumstances, to preserve his plans and reputation, Orikan is forced to employ a closely guarded set of chronomantic abilities. Travelling backwards down his own timeline, he emerges in the past at a point at which he can set his prophesied version of the future back on track, normally by having the interfering factor destroyed in some manner.

In Orikan's predictions, the Imperial Navy dockyards on Helios VI should never have survived the onset of Waaagh! Skullkrak, and did so only by an inconvenient intervention by the meddlesome Silver Skulls 4th Company. By retroactively arranging for the Space Marines to be ambushed and nearly wiped out by Necron forces some weeks earlier, Orikan ensured that the destruction of Helios VI ultimately occurred as first foreseen. Thus were the Necrons able to reclaim much of the surrounding sector, and more importantly, thus was Orikan's reputation kept intact.

Orikan has always been sparing of such actions, and rightly so, for his meddling can birth all manner of unforeseen events. As a direct result of the Helios VI affair, no less than five Space Marine Chapters, including the Death Spectres, Howling Griffons and the remainder of the Silver Skulls, descended upon the Lazar System to take revenge, utterly destroying the tomb world from whence Orikan's original commission had come. In that case, Orikan's culpability in the disaster remained secret, but it could have easily gone otherwise.

Orikan takes great care to keep his machinations hidden from his peers. Though chronomancy is a science practiced by many other Crypteks, no other is remotely capable of Orikan's feats, something that would increase a hundredfold the suspicion in which he is held. And suspicion is the last thing Orikan needs at this moment. A thousand millennia of planning and preparation are about to come to fruition. Once the stars are in the proper alignment, Orikan will finally embrace his true destiny; his physical form will become a vessel for impossible celestial energies, making him a shining being of terrible power, and the temporal traps he has set throughout the galaxy will activate – and, like a spider pulling at its web, Orikan will manipulate the skein of time itself to his advantage.

> *'Time is a weapon like any other. If nothing else, I can simply wait for my foes to rot.'*
>
> – Orikan the Diviner

# TRAZYN THE INFINITE
## ARCHEOVIST OF THE SOLEMNACE GALLERIES

Trazyn is a preserver of histories, artefacts and events. The vast and numberless vaults burrowed through the tomb world of Solemnace are crowded with technologies so rare and sublime that any Adeptus Mechanicus Tech-Priest would give the lives of several close colleagues just to know that they existed. It is a hoard ever growing, for history is always on the march and Trazyn strives to keep pace. Alas, not many worlds willingly give up the artefacts Trazyn seeks, selfishly clutching onto the few meaningful things in their civilisation rather than offering them up to be preserved through the ages. In such circumstances, Trazyn has little choice but to muster his armies and take them by force – if this results in the destruction of a city, a planet or an entire sector, so be it.

Most impressive of all Solemnace's wonders are the prismatic galleries, winding chambers of statuary recapturing events from history that Trazyn deems worthy of preservation. The prismatic galleries are populated not with mere sculpture, but living beings transmuted into hard-light holograms by arcane technology. Some such statues are nothing less than the original enactors of history, frozen in the moment of triumph or defeat and whisked away to Solemnace to forever stand as testament to their deeds. Occasionally a statue will be destroyed by cruel happenstance. Such events drive Trazyn to frustration, for he must halt his search for fresh acquisitions and seek out replacements.

Of course, few of the statues are replaceable, but there are no rules to Trazyn's galleries save those that he himself decides upon. If he decrees that one of the hard-light tableaus must fulfil its function with substitutes – however inaccurate – then he will acquire them. Fully one tenth of his 'Death of Lord Solar Macharius' gallery is populated by holographic Imperial Guardsmen whose uniforms are three hundred years astray from historical fact, but Trazyn cares more for the spectacle than the details. Once Trazyn has resolved to refresh his galleries, he does so with great urgency. Depending on the scale of losses, replenishment might be achieved by a few simple kidnappings by low-flying Night Scythes, or possibly through a more substantial mobilisation of force.

Nor are tomb worlds immune to Trazyn's attention. Trazyn makes little distinction between artefacts held on alien worlds and those possessed by his own kind. The resulting indiscreet 'liberations' have rendered him unwelcome on several tomb worlds. He is forbidden entirely from the catacombs of Mandragora under pain of death, and permitted on Moebius on the strict understanding that his arrival will only benefit the Nekthyst Dynasty.

That Trazyn is rarely discovered before he is ready to make his move says rather more about the insular nature and selective knowledge of other Necrons than it does his own aptitude for subterfuge. Even on Ork-held planets, Trazyn goes to great pains to keep his identity a secret. He knows full well that his activities have come to the attention of certain Rogue Traders and Inquisitors – after all, the Imperium's tangled history presents something of an irresistible lure. Nonetheless, while he remains confident in his ability to outwit the plots and snares of primitive humans, Trazyn's paranoia is still his true master.

Trazyn commonly conducts his campaigns through surrogates – substitute bodies into which he can pour his will. Should the body suffer catastrophic damage, Trazyn's essence simply returns to his 'true' form, or into another surrogate. Many of these are actually Necron Lords or Overlords in their own right who, unbeknownst to them, have had their bodies subverted by Trazyn. Should he need to occupy such a body, he can do so as easily as he could any other surrogate – the regular occupant's will is suppressed, and the body itself instantly morphs into an exact facsimile of his primary form. Yet these days of caution and plotting are fast passing by. The raucous din of war grows louder in every corner of the galaxy, consuming temples, cities, worlds and even entire races long before Trazyn has had the opportunity to catalogue and 'rescue' all that is worth saving. Thus, for the first time in millions of years, Trazyn is mobilising the full might of Solemnace – the better to secure entire planets from the onset of ignorant barbarians. Already a score of the Imperium's worlds are under occupation by Trazyn's forces, the inhabitants subjugated by his implacable minions, but the legions of Solemnace show no signs of stopping.

# NEMESOR ZAHNDREKH & VARGARD OBYRON

## GRAND HIGH MASTERS OF GIDRIM, NOBLE LORDS OF THE EASTERN FRINGE

Nemesor Zahndrekh was once counted amongst the greatest generals in the Necron dynasties. By his campaigns of conquest did the world of Gidrim rise from ruling a small and insignificant planet on the fringes of the galaxy, to the iron-handed governance of a dozen star systems. Even now, though Gidrim has been subsumed into the Sautekh Dynasty, Zahndrekh is numbered amongst the mightiest of heroes. It is a reputation well deserved, for Gidrim is one of the more expansionist of the recently awoken crownworlds, and Zahndrekh's armies are an ever-present peril upon the galaxy's eastern fringe.

Yet for all his military genius, Zahndrekh does not see reality as it truly is. His mind suffered damage during the Great Sleep, and as a consequence he is trapped deep in the past, in the Wars of Secession that wracked his corner of the dynasties. In his mind, he fights these campaigns still as a creature of flesh and blood, crushing rebellious kings and bringing their domains back into the fold. He does not see armies of Orks, Aeldari or Men, but hosts of rebellious kinsmen battling to sunder his beloved dynasties. As such, Zahndrekh is one of the few Necron Overlords to employ the full protocols of honourable war against all encroachers – where others see aliens, he sees only Necrontyr. He disdains the use of Deathmarks, assassin Wraiths and other strategies forbidden by the codes of battle – not that his subordinates have any such compunction. Wherever possible, Zahndrekh ensures that enemy commanders are captured, not killed, and thereafter treated as honoured prisoners – much to the outraged consternation of Zahndrekh's Royal Court.

Indeed, there are many Lords in Zahndrekh's Royal Court who would dearly love to see the old general removed from power, for they judge that his adrift perceptions greatly outweigh his feats of battle. However, as befits his station, Zahndrekh has formidable defences against regicide. His personal sepulchre is heavily woven with traps, his personal household retinue boasts three entire legions of Lychguard, and he even employs four-score food tasters – though it has been countless millennia since any morsel passed his lips. Yet Zahndrekh has one defence greater than all others – his aide and protector, Vargard Obyron.

Obyron served as Zahndrekh's vargard in their very first campaign – an undignified but hugely successful series of skirmishes in the swamps of Yama – and has stood steadfast at his side ever since, both on the field of battle and off it. Unlike his master, Obyron is very much aware of the changes wrought upon their existence, but has long since abandoned any attempt to awaken Zahndrekh to reality – whatever the fault in his master's mind, the damage lies too deep. So, like any dedicated servant, Obyron attends to all the loose ends created by Zahndrekh's eccentricities, chief

of which are seeing to it that 'honoured' prisoners of war are 'killed whilst trying to escape', and that upstart Lords of the Royal Court are either silenced or disposed of.

Obyron's instincts for Gidrim's politics are every bit as finely tuned as Zahndrekh's are for battle. It is quite impossible for any plot to mature without word of it reaching Obyron, at which point he takes action to ensure it dies. The exact method depends greatly on what Obyron considers to have the greatest impact. A public trial by combat for the chief plotter is invariably Obyron's favoured method – his skill with a blade, legendary long before biotransference, has decayed little with the passing millennia. Sometimes, however, Obyron deems the quiet terror of a conspirator's disappearance to have a more enduring effect. Regardless of method, Obyron has proven his supremacy hundreds of times over, yet every few decades, another upstart noble foolishly chances his arm against the Overlord of Gidrim who, for his part, is content to leave the vargard to his work. On many other worlds, Necron or otherwise, Obyron would be considered the true power behind the throne, yet his loyalty to Zahndrekh is total and completely without guile. He seeks no reward beyond continued service, and has never displayed an iota of desire to rule through his master.

On campaign, Zahndrekh and Obyron have proven to be an almost undefeatable combination. Zahndrekh seldom lowers himself to personal combat, but instead wields as a weapon the battlefield acumen that somehow remains undimmed by his faltering memory. Under his gaze, the Necron armies of Gidrim react almost instantaneously to counter enemy strategies, shifting between aggressive and defensive postures at a moment's notice. With a few carefully chosen words of command, outflanking foes are isolated and crushed, enemy assault waves dispersed, and fire support positions obliterated. Such is Zahndrekh's crystal-perfect reading of the flow of battle that even the enemy's experienced veterans often seem like raw and fumbling recruits as their every tactic is anticipated and their every skill countered.

> *'Another fine victory over the crude and the disorderly, Obyron! It seems strange to me that the enemy generals saw fit to loose so many wild beasts upon the field of battle. Their so-called tactics become more desperate and barbaric by the day. So long as we stand tall, old friend, it shall avail them naught. Onward!'*
> — Nemesor Zahndrekh to Vargard Obyron, following the defeat of Tyranid splinter fleet Mawgawr

For his part, Obyron fights in the front lines, wielding his warscythe with a precision to be expected of a warrior who counts his campaigns by the thousand. Yet no matter how distant he is, Obyron always keeps close watch on Zahndrekh – his responsibilities as bodyguard outweigh any other considerations. Should Zahndrekh be threatened, Obyron always returns to his master's side in a shadowy flicker of energy. His ghostwalk mantle is at all times locked on to the nemesor's homing algorithm; it can teleport him and those nearby back with utter reliability, allowing him to intervene in no time.

It is well that Obyron is so dedicated, for few Lords of Gidrim are eager to fight alongside their nemesor. Some simply cannot tolerate Zahndrekh's constant stream of reminiscences to battles fought long ago, relevant to the campaign at hand though those recollections always are. For others, Zahndrekh's damaged mind is a constant reminder of the fate that might one day be theirs, should need dictate they enter stasis-sleep once more. None of them sees that such damage has doubtless already been wrought – that they are, in truth, just as blind to their own involuntarily idiosyncrasies as Zahndrekh is to his own.

It speaks much to Zahndrekh's skills – and, perhaps more crucially, those of Obyron – that despite the peculiarities in his tactics and his strict adherence to the Triarch's ancient codes of honour, he remains one of Imotekh's finest generals. Together, Zahndrekh and Obyron form a bulwark against the teeming hordes of disorder that would encroach upon the Sautekh Dynasty

Nemesor Zahndrekh stared dolefully at the seething tide of greenskins that was tumbling over the canyon edge opposite. Some of the armoured brutes died on impact, with the Necron warriors firing up at them from the bottom of the gulch. Many more struck axe-first, their crunching impact causing the Necrons to phase out by the score.

'These separatists are insane,' said Zahndrekh with a chattering sigh of exasperation. 'They were supposed to be trapped at the edge of the cliff, not to voluntarily jump over it. Our fine plan lies in tatters, Obyron.'

The hulking vargard said nothing, for his emerald gaze was on the skies. There was a sudden roar, and a trio of Orks hurtled upon smoking jetpacks, bellowing as they fired their primitive pistols at the nemesor. Obyron blinked from existence to reappear in the path of the bullets. They ricocheted from the bodyguard's impervious metal body without harm. The Ork jump troops thundered down, brandishing their axes. Obyron's scythe flashed once, twice, three times. Six bleeding lumps of Ork flesh fell to the ground nearby. Their blood spattered the nemesor, but he did not notice, for he was intent on the battle in the gulch.

'Nothing for it,' said Zahndrekh. 'Send in the Monoliths, and have the Night Scythes bring in the reserve phalanxes in a classic Ectos overlap. We can still be back in time for the feast!'

# ANRAKYR THE TRAVELLER
## LORD OF THE PYRRHIAN LEGIONS

Few Necrons awaken from stasis-sleep with a fully functioning consciousness. Most arise addled by the long slumber, their wits and reason slow to come fully online. Not so Anrakyr – he rose from dormancy with his mind intact and a great purpose foremost within it: to reunite the dynasties. Embracing this as his destiny, Anrakyr abdicated all responsibility to his own tomb world of Pyrrhia and led an army into the stars.

Yet the galaxy has changed much since Anrakyr last walked its worlds, and the maps of old no longer correspond with the reality of the present. Planets have been destroyed, isolated by warp storms or even shifted through time and space. Even should the world itself remain in the position recorded, the tomb beneath its surface might well be gone, destroyed by tectonic upheaval, meteor strike or other unforeseen disaster. Worst of all, however, is for Anrakyr to arrive upon a sleeping tomb world to discover it infested with lesser life forms.

Anrakyr has little desire to start war for its own sake – his forces are too meagre for wanton hostility – but to arrive on a slumbering tomb world to discover its catacombs collapsed and its resources plundered is enough to drive him into an abiding rage that bodes ill for the perpetrators. Be the invaders a low-tech colony, a sprawling Waaagh! of Orks, a T'au expeditionary force or the planet-choking industries of the Adeptus Mechanicus, only one response is possible: total war – fighting alongside the tomb world's forces if any remain, battling to avenge them if not. Not all the tomb worlds Anrakyr arrives upon are in such dire throes, but in a galaxy burgeoning with inquisitive life, uncontested planets are few and far between.

From each tomb world awoken or freed from invaders, Anrakyr requests a tithe of warriors and weaponry to be given to his cause. If he is refused, he seizes his prize through force or artifice instead. A newly awakened tomb world is inevitably a confused and disordered place, and such acquisitions are easily engineered. This practice has earned the Traveller a dubious reputation in the eyes of some among the dynasties. While to many he is considered the highest avatar of nobility, a warrior who has yielded personal rank and status for the benefit of his people, to others, Anrakyr is the worst kind of masterless brigand, almost as severe a threat to the slumbering tomb worlds as any of the galaxy's other perils.

On the battlefield, Anrakyr is often accompanied by a cadre of his Pyrrhian Eternals – the remnant of the vast Immortal legion with which he began his great work. These ageless veterans are utterly faithful to their master and murderously efficient in furthering his goals. Yet even their threat pales beside that of Anrakyr himself. When he desires that an enemy be utterly destroyed, he unleashes the power of his tachyon arrow, a wrist-mounted energy caster. When fired, this device utilises faster-than-light tachyonic particles to transmute a sliver of metal into a lance of energy that can erase a foe from existence entirely.

The same force of will that enables Anrakyr to maintain command over his forces can be refocused to deceive enemy targeting systems, granting him control of the foe's weaponry for brief periods of time. So it is that any foe who takes the field against Anrakyr would be well served to pay equal attention to the guns at their rear in addition to those at their front...

> 'I am not capricious, nor am I given to cruel acts for their own sakes. It is simply a fact that you and your kind have trespassed, and thus invited extermination. Curse you for putting me to this inconvenience.'
>
> - Anrakyr the Traveller to T'au Ethereal Aun'Taniel,
> prior to the Harvest of Ka'mais

# WARRIORS

Necron Warriors form the cold heart of a tomb world's armies. They are implacable, emotionless and terrifying – the inexorable emissaries of death itself. Yet on closer inspection, faults become visible that act against the Warrior's image of the reaper. Its reactions, though precise, are slow. Its limbs, though strong and sleek, are pitted and corroded, covered with an oily fluid seeping from aged joints. Its movements are jerky, and every so often it stumbles as synapses misfire. The Necron Warrior would almost be pitiable were it not for the merciless gleam flickering in its eyes and the pervasive sense that it is less a sentient creature than it is one of the walking dead.

Necron Warriors are in no way autonomous. They are bound entirely to their commander's unyielding will. Outside of simple instructions, their tactical awareness is almost entirely non-existent, and without more specific orders a phalanx of Warriors automatically settles into a guard routine, repelling enemy attacks with rippling volleys of precision gauss fire. All this they do in utter silence, for vocalisation was a luxury deliberately denied them by design.

What Necron Warriors lack in intuition they more than make up for in determination and durability. Once orders have been received, they are completely single-minded and will follow commands through to conclusion without question. Furthermore, individual warriors can suffer grievous damage before they cease fighting. Even dismemberment or decapitation may not stay a Necron Warrior's advance, for its sophisticated self-repair mechanisms can return it to the fray. Despite this incredible endurance, a Necron Warrior is not entirely fearless. Though most of its instincts have long since been expunged or degraded into nothingness, its need for self-preservation still has some purchase on its mind. Should this survival instinct go untriggered, however, the Warrior will carry on fighting to almost unbelievable degrees, marching heedlessly through the worst horrors of war.

It is possible that the Necron Warriors' paucity of wit and self-identity are side-effects of the biotransference process. In the Time of Flesh they were not soldiers, but citizens of lesser status. It was inevitable that their conversion would be neither so careful nor so precise as that of the Necron soldiery or royalty. Even more disturbing is the idea that the Necron Warriors might have been deliberately stripped of awareness by the nobles, thus ensuring they would serve as loyal foot soldiers in the battles to come.

## GAUSS WEAPONRY

Gauss weapons are the mainstay arms of the Necron legions, ranging from the rifle-sized gauss flayer through to the enormous heavy gauss cannon. No matter their scale, the function of these weapons is the same; they emit a molecular disassembling beam, capable of reducing flesh, armour and bone to their constituent atoms in a moment. Even the thick armour plating of an Astra Militarum tank is no proof against such horrendous firepower. The awful wounds caused by gauss weapons are greatly feared by the line infantry of the other races, and are almost impossible to treat using conventional methods.

# IMMORTALS

When the Necrons first conquered the galaxy, they did so through the unfaltering and implacable onslaught of legion upon legion of Immortals. These were the very elite of the Necrontyr armies, hardened veterans born anew in tireless metal bodies. For hundreds of years, the Immortals were a scourge upon all who stood between the Necrons and galactic domination. Now, the Immortal legions are but an echo of what they once were, for countless trillions were destroyed in the final days of the War in Heaven. Yet billions more survived, and now wait only to be awakened from their tombs and begin the reconquest of the galaxy.

As the shock troops of a tomb world's armies, Immortals have a far wider range and depth of reaction than Necron Warriors, for they have retained much of their tactical and strategic experience. Indeed, in many ways the transfer to machine bodies and minds only sharpened the Immortals' ability to prosecute war in an efficient fashion. Left to their own devices, a phalanx of Immortals continues to strive for victory using every tactic and stratagem at their disposal. This is not to say that Immortals do not have shortcomings. Most profound is the fact that they are incapable of learning and adapting to new means of battle. On the rare occasions when Immortals are presented with a battlefield situation that cannot be conquered by ancient tactics, they will apply the counter-strategy they consider the closest match, regardless of its ultimate suitability. Fortunately, such instances are unusual for, no matter the advances in technology, war has changed little since the days of the War in Heaven.

Immortals are capable of speech, albeit in flat and emotionless tones that are even more soulless than the hollow voices of the Overlords. This enables them to not only provide clinically precise battlefield reports to their superiors, but also to issue orders to Necron Warriors, a factor that often increases the efficiency of the entire battlefront. Outside these parameters, Immortals are, at best, limited conversationalists, often falling prey to recursive loops of logic and procedure in place of conveying any pertinent information. If presented with an enquiry or concept beyond its understanding, an Immortal simply does not respond. This trait only serves to encourage the more arrogant Necron Overlords in their rambling and rhetorical soliloquies. This, in turn, ensures that a nemesor's pre-battle address to his troops can drag on for an interminably long time, as he scours his Immortals' silent forms for some glimmer of understanding and they, with patience born of utter incomprehension, stare straight back at him, waiting solemnly for the order that will throw them into battle once more.

What Immortals lack in flexibility of approach, they more than make up for in durability and firepower. Immortals are more thickly armoured than Necron Warriors and can weather a storm of heavy bolter or assault cannon fire with little more to show for it than fresh carbon-scoring on their already time-worn frames. Even should an Immortal be felled, its threat is not ended, for its auto-repair systems are, if anything, the tiniest fraction more efficient than that of the baseline warriors. Few foes can withstand the Immortals' return fire so easily. A single shot from a gauss blaster can punch through most types of armour to strip flesh from bone, and the closer the Immortals come to their target, the shorter the interval between blistering volleys. At that point, all the foe can do is dive for cover, but this offers only a fool's hope of survival. There can be no hiding from Immortals – their gauss blasters will scour every nook and cranny until naught remains but ash on the breeze.

## TESLA WEAPONRY

Some of the most terrifying weapons deployed by the warriors of the Necron dynasties utilise tesla technology. Such armaments unleash bolts of living lightning that envelop their target, melting flesh and metal alike. Worse still for the victim, these bolts feed off the energy unleashed by this destruction, growing more and more furious with each volley.

The bulkiest tesla weapons – such as the much-feared tesla destructor carried by Night Scythes and Annihilation Barges – fire crackling arcs that not only immolate the target instantaneously, but create forks of searing energy that reach out to strike other victims.

# LYCHGUARD

In ancient times, Lychguard were the wardens of the nobility, said to be incorruptible and utterly dedicated to their charges. Then, such an assertion was as much propaganda as it was truth. Though the Lychguard doubtless possessed greater loyalty than the common run of soldiery, they were still but mortal and prone to all the temptations and weaknesses to which flesh is heir. Now, Lychguard are indeed that which legend made them. They are no longer capable of straying from their master's edicts – careful engram manipulation during biotransference saw to that. Each is programmed with unswerving loyalty to a particular noble, or sometimes to a whole dynasty. This, combined with the fact that they have retained most of their personality intact, makes Lychguard the ideal emissaries and lieutenants in situations deemed too dangerous to risk the existence of a phaeron or his regal subordinates.

Physically, Lychguard are incredibly imposing, housed in the same heavily armoured forms more commonly reserved for Necron royalty. This is mostly due to practicality – after all, what use is a bodyguard if he has not might and hardiness enough to defend his master? However, there is also an underlying arrogance to the Lychguard's exceptionally resilient design, a brazenness meant to present an irresistible challenge to the noble's enemies. Accordingly, Lychguard can inevitably be found at the heart of any battle, either because their master's army has rallied around them, or the enemy has chosen to make the destruction of their charge a priority.

As with much of the Necron army, a Lychguard's armament is decreed largely by tradition. Most are equipped with heavy-bladed warscythes drawn from their patron's personal armoury – when combined with a Lychguard's prodigious strength, there is very little such a blade cannot penetrate. Phalanxes employed by more influential Overlords instead carry hyperphase swords and dispersion shields, trading a little in the way of raw strength in favour of the incredible protection granted by the dispersion shields' interlocking force barriers. Whilst such a squad might make slower progress as they carve through a Space Marine strike force, the ability to withstand anything from a siege shell to a defence laser blast is ample compensation.

With the exception of the gore-maddened Novokh Slaughterers, each dynasty's Lychguard favours single, dismembering strikes over flurries of lesser blows, trusting their own hardiness to hold the enemy at bay. Unlike lesser Necrons, Lychguard take pride in – and even relish – their bloody work. Indeed, for a Lychguard, anything less than a perfect strike is something to be regretted. Some Lychguard even go so far as to seek forgiveness from their sovereign if they land anything less than an immaculate stroke. So will a Lychguard sometimes stand motionless in the heat of battle, its blade raised and unmoving whilst it awaits the most auspicious moment to strike. When that moment arrives, the Lychguard brings its blade about in an unstoppable arc to sever limbs, lop heads or cleave torsos in two.

## BLADES OF THE PHAERONS

The majority of Necron close-combat weapons, such as the warscythes carried by the elite Lychguard, project destabilising energy fields that warp and buckle armour. Other weapons, like the deadly hyperphase sword, vibrate at such a tremendous frequency that they shift between several dimensional states, passing straight through shields and thick chitin plating to sink into the victim's vital organs.

# TOMB BLADES

The Tomb Blade was originally designed as a void-capable, single-pilot fighter during the final days of the War in Heaven. As Necrons' robotic bodies are immune to the hazards of interplanetary space, traditional pressure-sealed and canopied craft were unnecessary from the very outset. Acting in flights that were dozens or even hundreds strong, Tomb Blades would swarm over enemy capital ships, overwhelming armour and weapon systems with waves of pinpoint gauss and tesla fire. So successfully did the craft perform in its primary environment that modified versions soon appeared in planet-side battles. Over time this became the more commonplace of the two roles, one of the few occasions in which the hidebound traditions of the Necron military were adapted to exploit opportunity.

The Tomb Blade has a curious motion for a craft of its design, eschewing the arrow-straight attack vectors of other jetbikes and fighter craft. The attack craft's dimensional repulsor engines ensure that gravity, momentum and other forces have little purchase upon its frame. As a result, the craft often corkscrew across the battlefield rather than taking a more direct approach, and constantly change vectors and altitude in a manner fit to boggle the enemy's aim. No flesh and blood pilot could ever hope to contend with such an anarchic approach without succumbing to blackouts and nausea, but such hazards have no hold over machines.

Despite appearances to the contrary, the attack patterns performed by Tomb Blades are strictly controlled by a series of hyper-fractal equations. Indeed, they.have to be, for a Necron Warrior alone would make for a truly dreadful pilot. To compensate for this, attack patterns are entirely pre-planned and the pilot cannot alter them once in flight, though it can switch between different tactical packages in order to adapt to fresh objectives.

The pre-programmed nature of a Tomb Blade's flight means that it is therefore theoretically possible to predict the flight path it will take, but only a genius-level intellect could divine that there was a pattern at all. Even if said genius could isolate and identify the particular set of equations in use, no conventional targeting computer could ever hope to process the data fast enough to be of any help. Some Tomb Blades are even fitted with shadowlooms that emit a veil of unnatural darkness to shroud the vehicle, making their esoteric flight-paths even more difficult to track. Thus, a Tomb Blade is just as difficult a quarry as the most accomplished of all mortals, even though its pilot's skill is immensely inferior.

Tomb Blades often operate far ahead of the main army, striking at lightly defended positions, supply convoys and other targets of opportunity. Though the planet-side version of these craft do not mount the macro-class hull-cutter weaponry of the space-fighter variants, the twinned tesla carbines and gauss blasters can prove just as devastating when employed against advancing infantry. When deployed against entrenched enemy positions, many Tomb Blades carry nebuloscopes, allowing them to trace M-dimensional paths along which they can fire upon their targets. Others – particularly those serving as a vanguard force against heavy enemy defences – are arrayed with shieldvanes, affording them additional protection as they conduct their withering strafing runs.

# DEATHMARKS

For countless millennia, Deathmark squads have served the Necrons nobility as snipers and assassins. Even when they were beings of flesh and blood, Deathmarks had a reputation for cold-hearted precision and patience. Now, housed in tireless metal bodies, Deathmarks are more deadly than they ever were in the Time of Flesh.

Whilst Deathmarks are as much part of a tomb world's army as Immortals and Necron Warriors, tradition dictates strict rules concerning their use. As agents of assassination and ambush, ancient codes forbid the deployment of Deathmarks in wars between the nobility, or against other 'honourable' enemies. Only the Nekthyst regularly flaunt this code, further cementing their dubious reputation. Luckily, as most alien foes are considered far from worthy until they have had a chance to prove otherwise on the battlefield, and few enemy commanders encounter Deathmarks and live to tell the tale, this gives all but the most traditional and hidebound nemesors carte blanche to employ these assassins against practically any alien they see fit.

Deathmarks seldom take position with the rest of the army at battle's start. Instead, they slip sideways out of reality and monitor the ongoing conflict from a hyperspace oubliette – a pocket dimension riding the gap between then and now. They can remain here for days upon end, waiting patiently for the opportune moment to act. Deathmarks choose their time of intercession carefully. They can be summoned to the fray at the order of the army's commander, but more often they are left to employ their own judgement – biotransference has done little to dull the Deathmarks' predatory instincts and most nemesors are content to trust to this. From their hyperspace sanctuary, the Deathmarks can track the initiation and target points of enemy communication channels, teleport beams and even orbital descents with childish ease. Thus are the deployment locations of enemy commanders and reinforcements betrayed.

With the target tracked and established, the Deathmarks exit their oubliette to appear silently upon a ridge or ruin that affords unobstructed view of their quarry. From here, the Deathmarks place the hunter's mark from which they take their name – an

eerie green energy halo that plays about the target's head. The halo glows brightly through five dimensions, ensuring that no matter how far or by what manner the target flees, the Deathmarks will never lose track of them. Naturally, such a marking does not last forever, perhaps only an hour or so at best, but an hour is a laughably long time for a Deathmark squad on the hunt. The target will be lucky to survive more than a few seconds before being torn apart by fire from the Deathmarks' long-barrelled synaptic disintegrators.

The weapons of the Deathmarks kill the mind as well as the body. Not only do these strange glowing rifles fire a pulse of energy powerful enough to scorch flesh to ash, they also break apart the neural pathways that enable sentient creatures to think, to

act, even to breathe. Each shot essentially slices the brain in a million different locations at once; regardless of which part of the body the shot actually strikes, their baleful emanations will reach the target's brain in some manner or another, cutting away their thoughts – severing their very sentience – to leave the victim with no chance of recovery. It is fortunate indeed that these undying warriors have suffered their own mental degenerations, or they would never miss.

> 'Once you are marked, there is no escape.'
>
> - Illic Nightspear,
> Master of Pathfinders

# DESTROYER LORDS

Not all Necrons awaken from the great sleep as hale as was intended. Some suffer physical damage in the intervening millennia; usually faulty stasis-crypts bring on a slow decay that rots the mechanical body and erodes engrammic pathways. Others become infected by the flayer virus and devolve into creatures whose reason is subsumed by a taste for flesh. Yet there are also those Necrons who awaken from slumber with their physical form intact but their psyche torn beyond recovery. Angered and despairing of their soulless existence, these Necrons turn to nihilism. They no longer seek redemption or repatriation with the flesh that was so long lost to them. They wish only to drive all other living things into death's welcoming embrace. These are the Destroyers, the self-appointed heralds of oblivion.

Destroyer Lords are the most maniacal of their kind. This is chiefly because they retain far more intellect than baseline Destroyers, and can bring all of this fearsome intelligence to bear in their pursuit of galactic conquests. This efficiency is all the more murderous for the Destroyer Lord's complete lack of empathy. Whilst few Necrons retain any instinctive comprehension of pity and mercy, the cleverest amongst them can at least still grasp such concepts intellectually. Not so Destroyer Lords – they have long ago discarded any ability to empathise with other creatures. If a Destroyer Lord takes prisoners, it is not out of honour or pity, but simple efficiency. There are a thousand ways in which captives can be used as lures for other fleshlings, and Destroyer Lords are conversant with every last one.

In a galaxy full to overspilling with genocidal despots, Destroyer Lords remain worthy of mention as something truly horrific. Those of the Mephrit Dynasty, whose culture prizes obliteration above all others, are particularly well known for systematically annihilating entire systems, planet by planet, leaving only corpse-strewn wastelands behind them. Where others kill for pleasure, or in service to some malignant god, Destroyer Lords pursue their bloody crusade simply because it is their chosen course. By their calculation, joy is just one more pointless emotion, and the favour of gods naught but a crutch to support the frailties of flesh.

In truth, even Overlords find Destroyer Lords somewhat disconcerting, believing them to have too willingly embraced the machine. Most also hold the lingering suspicion that when all organic life has been eliminated, their nihilistic brethren will turn on their own kind. As a result, many Destroyer Lords are outcasts. Stripped of rank, they are forced to dwell on the periphery of Necron civilisation, lest their madness prove infectious.

Destroyer Lords are formidable combatants, for their physical strength equals that of the mightiest Overlords. Many favour warscythes or voidblades over ranged tools of war. In his horrific way, a Destroyer Lord is a craftsman, and the fruits of his bloody labours are far more easily tallied in the thick of the fighting. There is no artistry to a Destroyer Lord's blows – each swing of his blade is driven by the desire for optimum efficiency. Similarly, those few that do favour slaughtering from afar train their deathly beams upon their enemies with cold, dispassionate precision. The resultant annihilation – though often spectacular – is registered by the Destroyer Lord simply as the logical conclusion of their hardwired hatred.

Indeed, the obliterative drive of a Destroyer Lord is so potent that their mere presence on the battlefield rouses lesser Destroyers. So amplified, they are able to achieve even greater acts of wanton carnage as they carry out their master's wrathful plans.

# DESTROYERS

Destroyers are deranged agents of annihilation whose sole reason for existence is centred around an unshakeable yearning to quench the flames of life. A Destroyer cares not for borders or allegiance, nor does he make any distinction between the innocent and the damned – all life is his enemy, and all living creatures are his prey.

It is not the Destroyers' violent madness alone that makes them so different from the other denizens of a tomb world. Insanity infects many a slumbering Necron, though it rarely takes a dramatic form, but instead merely exacerbates the victim's innate eccentricities. Yet even the lowliest Necron Warrior longs for a return to the Time of Flesh, and because its physical form echoes the living, breathing, soulful creature it once was, it will under no circumstances tolerate further dilution or corruption of that physical form. Instead, for a Destroyer, everything is subsumed into the all-important goal of annihilation. They ruthlessly adapt, augment or expunge any facet of their physical form if it will improve their mission of slaughter. Legs are removed in favour of repulsor platforms, arms

are fused to the workings of gauss cannons. Even the Destroyer's senses are reconfigured to better serve target-lock and prediction capability, its neural circuitry repathed to improve response times at the cost of vestigial emotions. None of this is to say that Destroyers do not feel fear; though they might explain a retreat away as conserving resources, it is a retreat nonetheless, spurred on by a spark of self-preservation that will never quite be extinguished.

What makes the rise of the Destroyers truly disturbing is that they can be found on almost every tomb world, from the poorest fringeworld to the noblest of crownworlds. This suggests that the descent into this particular form of madness is driven by subconscious imperative – possibly one implanted by the C'tan during biotransference. This does not mean that Destroyers hail from every level of Necron society. It takes a certain freedom of personality to embrace nihilism with such cold-blooded determination, a level of individuality denied to low-ranking Necrons. Destroyers therefore, almost without exception, emerge from the ranks of Immortals, Lychguard and, occasionally,

Deathmarks. Most are banished to the outskirts of their tomb world, dwelling in isolated fortresses ruled over by courts of Destroyer Lords.

A Destroyer's chilling dedication to destruction is a valuable addition to any Necron army. On most campaigns, their brutal efficiency more than compensates for the almost habitual insubordination with which they treat other Necrons of all ranks. The canniest and most thorough nemesors make a direct point of building campaigns around the actions of Destroyers, rather than making doomed attempts to enforce their own battle plan on the twisted warriors. So long as a Destroyer knows that there are other forms of life in the vicinity, it will direct its baleful attention upon their destruction, and has no intellect or focus to spare for such irrelevancies as orders and strategy. Once the enemy is in sight, Destroyers pay little or no heed to their allies, but instead settle into optimised and self-sufficient extermination patterns, shattering enemy formations with long range salvoes of gauss fire before moving into point-blank range to methodically scour survivors from the blackened craters.

# FLAYED ONES

Flayed Ones are carrion creatures, the victims of a terrible madness that took root during the last days of the War in Heaven. Their curse was the parting gift of one of the C'tan: *Llandu'gor*, the Flayer. It is said that when the Necrons turned upon the C'tan, the Flayer was not merely splintered as were his brothers, but utterly obliterated. Yet, in his dying moments, he called down a terrible curse upon his betrayers, tainting them with an echo of his fearsome hunger. For aeons the Flayer's curse went unnoticed and unseen. By the time the madness began to manifest, the afflicted Necrons had travelled far and wide, unwittingly spreading the disease to countless worlds.

A Necron over whom the flayer curse has taken hold suffers a slow and tortuous erosion of sanity. It begins to revel in the bloody ruin of fleshed foes, and is driven to claim gruesome trophies of skin, sinew and bone. As the madness progresses, the victim becomes compelled to feast upon the fallen. It cannot actually digest or consume flesh in any sense – the blood simply seeps through the gaps in its exoskeleton to clog its joints and pool at its feet – yet still the Necron is driven to gorge itself upon gore in a doomed attempt to sate an unquenchable lust. Physical changes occur shortly thereafter, wracking and twisting the afflicted Necron's form into something as warped in body as it is in function. Ultimately, the accursed Necron simply disappears, drawn by unknown instinct to a pocket dimension where he will forever dwell amidst the charnel palaces of the Flayed Ones. It is said only the Oroskh know the reason why.

Other Necrons loathe the Flayed Ones and fear them for the disease they carry. As a result, those suspected of infection are banished or destroyed before the affliction becomes contagious. However, no manner of precaution can prevent a pack of Flayed Ones joining a battle already underway. They can materialise at any time, lured from their bleak dimension by the scent of blood and carnage. Flayed Ones commonly attack with little regard for strategy, though they will occasionally have the presence of mind not to attack immediately, stalking their target until it is vulnerable. This is best done from downwind, as Flayed Ones are wreathed in a dense stench of rotting flesh. When the moment to

attack comes, Flayed Ones strike without hesitation, slashing at their prey with twisted talons and keening shrill madness. If the enemy flees, Flayed Ones rarely pursue, choosing instead to feast upon their victims. However, if the enemy proves particularly resilient, the Flayed Ones inevitably retreat, skittering into the shadows to await a more tractable target.

Most Overlords make little or no attempt to adapt their plans for the unwanted actions of Flayed Ones, preferring rather to accept any advantage their presence brings. Regardless of the horrific creatures' usefulness, it is not uncommon for an Overlord to order the execution of any surviving Flayed Ones at battle's end. Alas, only the most insane are slaughtered easily. The rest slip sideways through the dimensions to reappear in their palaces of rotting flesh, laden with their newly claimed trophies and reeking of fresh blood.

> 'We long ago removed our bodies from mortality's grasp and bartered away our souls for technological baubles and the trappings of power. Our minds, then, are all that remain for us to lose, and it is here that the next stroke against us will fall.
>
> Though our individual afflictions may take different forms, sooner or later we will all be lost to madness.'
>
> - *Szarekh,
> Last of the Silent Kings*

'That we, in our arrogance, believed that Humankind was first amongst the races of this galaxy will be exposed as folly of the worst kind

# TRIARCH PRAETORIANS

In the Necron dynasties, the Praetorians held the responsibility of maintaining the Triarch's rule, to ensure that wars and politics alike were pursued according to ancient codes. As such, they acted outside the political structures, and held both the right and the means to enforce their will should a Lord, Overlord or even a phaeron's behaviour contravene the edicts of old. However, the Triarch Praetorians also held a higher responsibility: to ensure that the Necron dynasties never fell, that their codes of law and order did not vanish into the darkness. In this, they failed. To all intents and purposes, the War in Heaven saw the destruction of the Necron dynasties. Though the Triarch Praetorians fought at the forefront of that cataclysm, their efforts were not enough. That shame hung heavy on the survivors and drove them to forsake hibernation. As the final sparks of the War in Heaven burnt out, the last Triarch Praetorians withdrew to the Necrontyr's ancient seats of power on the northern rim, preserving what they could from the vengeance of the Aeldari.

From their concealed fortresses, the Triarch Praetorians plotted for that day, many millennia distant though it was, when the Necrons would emerge to dominate the galaxy once again. Yet they knew there was a good chance that the untested stasis technology would fail, and that their sleeping kin would never wake. So it was that the Triarch Praetorians came to travel widely throughout the galaxy, masquerading as grim-faced gods on countless primitive worlds. They brought the codes of the Necrontyr to credulous primitives, reshaping cultures according to their own ideals. Few civilisations wholly embraced the Triarch Praetorians' teachings; many more were exterminated by wars, natural disaster or the vengeful outriders of Craftworld Alaitoc, who sought to undo the works of the Triarch whenever they could. Nonetheless, fragments of Triarch lore and archeotech survive on worlds not seen by Necron eyes in many thousands of years.

Now, as the Necrons stir ever more into wakefulness, the Triarch Praetorians have sensed an opportunity to expunge their failure. They are travelling across the galaxy, tomb world to tomb world, rebinding the sundered pieces of the Necron dynasties. It will be a long and interminably slow process, for the galaxy is vast beyond imagining, and the locations of many Necron worlds have been lost, but the Triarch Praetorians have patience enough for the search and a burning determination to see it done. Once a tomb world has been contacted and bound into the newly founded dynasties, a host of Triarch Praetorians is assigned to that world in perpetuity, to govern its protocols and act in its defence. So it is that formations of Triarch Praetorians are often found at a battle's forefront in the defence against invaders and campaigns of reclamation alike. Even could he do so, no noble would refuse such assistance, for extreme age has little dulled a Triarch Praetorian squad's combat skills.

Triarch Praetorians seldom fight in a battle's initial waves, preferring to hover above the fray on gravity displacement packs. From here they watch carefully, not only for the moment at which their intercession will have the most impact, but also to observe the foe's actions. Though Triarch Praetorians share the usual Necron contempt for any race that is not their own, they are ever watchful for an opponent marked millennia ago by their influence, and sometimes proclaim such creatures honourable foes against whom the codes of battle must be observed. This can prove frustrating to an army's commander – such niceties are unwelcome impedance to the battle's prosecution – but it would be a bold nemesor indeed who overruled the wishes of a Triarch Praetorian.

# TRIARCH STALKERS

Like an enormous mechanical spider, a Triarch Stalker picks its way over the battlefield, underslung weapon systems sending destructive energies left and right. Its slicing limbs and devastating weapons are controlled by a high-ranking Triarch Praetorian pilot that sits aloft, staring down with cool judgement upon those mortal weaklings that scurry before him. Though many a Necron noble makes use of anti-gravitic technology to better survey the field, it has long been tradition for these Triarch agents to ride multi-legged war constructs, and Necrons value tradition most highly. In practice, such adherence to ancient mores does not affect their efficacy on the field of battle. When a Triarch Stalker advances, it does so with a speed and surety that belies its jerking gait. Indeed, it can cover all manner of terrain with a deftness and precision seldom found in the walkers of less advanced races.

While the Triarch Stalker can mount a wide array of anti-infantry and anti-armour weaponry, it is most commonly employed as a dedicated tank-hunter that roams far ahead of the main army. Able to navigate dense jungle and mountainous terrain as swiftly and sure-footedly as open plains, Triarch Stalkers can easily outmanoeuvre more cumbersome tracked vehicles, the better to stay out of the enemies' vision while finding an ideal firing position. As such attacks are much more effective when the enemy is taken unawares, Triarch Stalkers rarely indulge in sustained fusillades. Instead, they prefer to employ hit-and-run tactics, launching one or two salvoes of fire and then skittering away into the shadows before the enemy can react to their threat.

On those occasions when a Triarch Stalker is deployed in the heart of the Necron battle lines, its main function is to provide close fire support, and it is typically equipped with a heat ray – a multipurpose fusion weapon. If an enemy tank stalls the attack, one focused blast from the Triarch Stalker's heat ray will cripple the target's capabilities. Similarly, if dug-in enemy infantry is hampering the Necron advance, a Triarch Stalker can break the deadlock. The pilot simply sets the heat ray to dispersed beam, and sends clouds of scorching plasma swirling into every crevasse to broil the enemy alive.

Should the Triarch Stalker's firepower prove insufficient to the task at hand, it can instruct nearby Necron phalanxes to add their firepower to its own, and even transmit targeting data to ensure these augmentative volleys are as accurate as possible. Only the toughest and bravest of foes can withstand such a barrage – others are driven screaming from the battlefield, or mown down by the pinpoint salvoes. The Charnovokh Dynasty places a high value upon the Triarch Stalkers that move amongst its disparate ranks; not only do these long-limbed constructs act as bastions of order and lawfulness amongst an essentially patchwork dynasty, they literally coordinate the efforts of the Necrons that march to war around them, binding them into coherent assaults.

Such a difference does a Triarch Stalker's presence make that habitual foes of the Necrons have learnt to prioritise its destruction. To guard against the retaliative strikes of the foe, each Triarch Stalker is protected by layered quantum shielding. Though a determined assault can still breach these fields, they can confound most energy attacks – and even solid shot weaponry – by sapping the energy of the incoming attack and transmuting it into a harmless equivalent. This normally buys the Triarch Stalker enough time to redeploy. With their durability thus enhanced, Triarch Stalkers are increasingly deployed at the head of vanguard forces, there to bear the brunt of the enemy's counter-attack until the main body of the Necron army reaches the battle zone.

# GHOST ARKS

There have been Ghost Arks since the very earliest days of the Necrontyr. Then, they were simple wooden carriages pulled by toiling beasts of burden, commissioned by families of the dead to convey corpses from their homes to their place of interment. Thousands of years later, at the time of biotransference, the now-motorised Ghost Arks took on darker connotations. Guided by grim-faced soldiers, they prowled the streets of the great cities. No longer was their business with the dead, but with the living, for they were the means by which unwilling citizens were dragged to the great transformative machines.

Though the leaders of the Necrontyr had pledged their allegiance to the C'tan, few of the common people wished for the change that was upon them. So did the Ghost Arks often convey the broken bodies of those beaten near unto death by the government's enforcers, for only a spark of life and memory was required for biotransference. As resistance grew, the Ghost Arks were crewed no longer by soldiers of flesh and blood, but by the first wave of converted Necrons; with that, all pretence at mercy and compassion ended. With each load of living cargo the Ghost Arks claimed, their reputation grew ever darker and their aspect ever more bleak. By the time biotransference was almost complete, the mere sight of a Ghost Ark was enough to provoke terror in those observers who could any longer feel such things. Those still living who saw the Ghost Arks about their work swore that the tortured souls of their victims flew thick about the wagons, haunting the air with mournful voices.

Much has changed for the Necrons in the countless millennia since, and the role of the Ghost Ark has changed with it. No longer the gaolers of the living, they are now the redeemers of the fallen, tasked with trawling the battlefields for remnants of Necrons no longer able to reconstruct themselves. Recovered components are then set upon by swarms of constructor scarabs. Working with near-silent efficiency, they return the fallen Necron to function if repairs are possible, or dissolve it into reusable raw energy if they are not. Repaired Necrons are then locked in stasis until the Ghost Ark is at capacity, at which point it will either return its salvaged cargo to their tomb world or else deploy them directly to the battlefield.

Ghost Arks are often pressed into service as conventional transport vehicles, conveying reinforcements to some vital area of the battlefield, or allowing Necron forces to attack from an unexpected quarter. The enemy's predicament is made all the worse by the fact that Necrons deployed in this fashion are, to all intents and purposes, accompanied by their own mobile repair station. Only by destroying the Ghost Ark can the foe have any hope of victory.

Since the coming of the Tyranid hive fleets to the Eastern Fringe, the Charnovokh Dynasty has fielded a great many Ghost Arks. The Overlords of the scattered Charnovokh holdings were swift to realise that where the Tyranids consumed all living tissue, much of the mineral bounty of their prey worlds were left behind. This knowledge was hard earned indeed; millions of Necrons lay shattered or maimed beyond self-recovery – or even phase parameters – across the lands of the Charnovokh realm. Instead of harnessing the mineral bounty of the dead worlds in the path of each bio-fleet to create new warriors, the Crypteks and Canoptek constructs of the dynasty built entire fleets of Ghost Arks from the wreckage of worlds stripped of biomass by the all-devouring swarms. Networks of these craft then combed the lifeless wastelands in exhaustive grid patterns, picking up the disembodied remains of fallen Necrons and reconstituting them into humanoid form once more. Necessity demanded that the Crypteks relax their reunification parameters, given the violence with which the swarms tore apart those who stood against them. As a result the legions of Necrons that lurch, reanimated, from the Charnovokh armada are as likely to be patchwork constructs as they are shining warriors of one hue.

> 'Immortality is not quite the same as invulnerability, but it is close enough.'
>
> - Illuminor Szeras,
> Cryptek Overseer of the
> Zantragora Conclave

# ANNIHILATION BARGES

Annihilation Barges are powerful anti-infantry support platforms. Each is armed with a linked pair of tesla destructors – enormous energy cannons that fire ferocious arcs of eldritch lightning. In their usual configuration, Annihilation Barges are set in fixed positions in the lowest and deepest sanctums of a Necron tomb. Should a group of intruders manage to circumvent the layers of traps, service robots and prowling Canoptek constructs, they will pass beneath the concealed emplacements in which the Annihilation Barges lie. An acrid discharge of emerald lightning later, and the interlopers are naught but dust upon the tomb's stale breezes.

When a Necron Overlord goes to war, the Annihilation Barges' ancient repulsor sleds are coaxed back into life and the vehicles add their firepower to the tomb world's army. They are especially popular amongst the forces of the Mephrit Dynasty; obsessed with obliterating the living, their phalanxes are keyed towards maximum destruction of enemy infantrymen and the beasts of war they sometimes goad to the front line. Annihilation Barges are seldom swift enough to keep pace with even the ponderous advance of the Necron army, and so they are often deployed as defences for strategic locations. From here they can counter enemy scout elements, without facing the risk of being swept aside by a concerted attack. Not only does this render valuable sectors of the battlefield immune to all but the most determined of enemy assaults, it ensures that the Annihilation Barges themselves are guaranteed to find bloody purpose. Additionally, most Overlords task a squad of Immortals or Necron Warriors as guards. Such a partnership can prove advantageous for both parties – the Annihilation Barge has a screen of allies to drive back incoming assaults, whilst its bodyguard benefits from massive firepower.

The Annihilation Barge's tesla destructors are primarily anti-personnel weapons, though only the most heavily armoured tanks can risk their wrath with utter impunity. The tesla destructor employs much the same lightning-arc technology as found in the smaller tesla cannons and carbines. Its energy discharges wreak terrible harm on living targets, searing their flesh and boiling their blood. Furthermore, the bolts will often leap from target to target before they are finally grounded, leaving a trail of smouldering carnage across a broad swathe of the battlefield.

Nowhere are Annihilation Barges more commonly employed than on the northern frontier planets of the Akannazad Dynasty. These tomb worlds are under perpetual assault from the Orks of Charadon, to whom the technology-rich and highly ordered Necron planets present an irresistible lure – both in terms of plunder and anarchic potential. Without the protection of Annihilation Barges, many of these worlds would have long ago been overrun. Few weapons other than the tesla destructor can wreak such efficient havoc amongst an oncoming Ork horde; its blast is powerful enough to shred the armour of Trukks and Looted Wagons, and when fired upon Ork boyz, lightning arcs wildly from one victim to the next, reducing flesh to ash.

## THE FALL OF THE TECHNOMANDRITES

Practically all of the Necrons' war machines owe provenance to a particular group of Crypteks: the Technomandrites of Magistrakh. This shadowy conclave stayed neutral during the First War of Secession, but sold their weaponeering knowledge to the highest bidder. The Technomandrites saw much profit from the spilt blood of their own kind, but it ultimately proved to be their undoing. When the Triarch's war against the Old Ones was first declared, the initial strike fell not against the aliens, but against Magistrakh. The reason the Silent King gave to the Necrontyr nobles was logical and compelling: if the Old Ones were to be defeated, no longer could one faction dictate the flow of arms. Yet this was, in part at least, a lie. Fear was the motivating force behind the Silent King's assault, fear that the Technomandrites' growing power would soon prove a challenge to the Triarch itself. Thus was the power of the Technomandrites broken forever. Those that remain are a but an echo of the past, and they dream of vengeance and restored glory.

# NIGHT SCYTHES

The Night Scythe is the Necrons' favoured tool of invasion, a variant of the Doom Scythe that foregoes some of the fighter's heaviest weaponry in favour of a troop transport capacity. This is not to say that the Night Scythe is in any way defenceless – quite the opposite. With its turret mounted tesla destructor, and the nerve-shredding shriek of its engines, the Night Scythe is still a formidable fighter craft in its own right.

Should a phaeron wish to reach out his hand and reclaim one of the sundered planets, his first wave of attack inevitably includes a fleet of Night Scythes. Manoeuvrable enough to evade incoming fire from orbital defence platforms and swift enough to outpace mustering defenders, Night Scythes can ghost through a defence perimeter to deploy invasion forces directly at the heart of key enemy installations and strategic locations. Once a foothold has been established, coordinates are relayed to the main army, enabling Monoliths and other forces to teleport into position, and the invasion to begin.

Unlike the armoured carriers employed by other races, the Night Scythe does not have a transport compartment as such. Instead, it deploys troops by means of a captive wormhole whose far end is anchored on a distant tomb world. Though this is less flexible than the Monolith's eternity gate, it does allow the Night Scythe to mimic the battlefield role of a more conventional transport vehicle without jeopardising the existence of its assigned squad. The Nephrekh Dynasty are the undisputed masters of this translocation technology, using such beams in every campaign. If a Night Scythe is destroyed, its payload squad is simply isolated from the battle until an alternate means of deployment can be established. Though this invariably prevents the squad from taking part in the immediate battle, this is preferable to them being destroyed outright.

Night Scythes are often employed as far-ranging scout ships, tasked with making contact with other tomb worlds or searching out lost Necron planets suitable for reclamation. On worlds where

the interlopers are either few in number or primitive in nature, the Night Scythe spearheads a ruthless subjugation. On worlds where other life forms have taken strong root, the pilot of the Night Scythe clandestinely performs probes and biopsies of the inhabitants, preying on isolated settlements or convoys whilst it searches for clues that will identify the inhabiting race's suitability for apotheosis. Such tests are long and exhaustive, and the pilot is often forced to dissect entire townships in order to harvest sufficient data.

On a particularly promising planet, the Night Scythe's pilot may go so far as to transport living samples back to its tomb world for further inspection by Crypteks. Most such subjects do not survive the scientific method, with many stripped down molecule by molecule and neuron by neuron. A few abductees are returned to their homes, but even these are implanted with mindshackle scarabs or other control mechanisms to enable them to function as unsuspecting spies and saboteurs who will pave the way for imminent invasion.

# DOOM SCYTHES

Doom Scythes are heralds of terror and dismay, supersonic fighter craft that range far ahead of a Necron invasion. Unlike many of the forces employed by the Necrons, Doom Scythes can function in a highly independent manner. Much of the craft's superstructure houses datastacks that are in turn heavily laden with strike plans, stratagems and tactical variants. When faced with a situation outside of known parameters, the pilot can sift through and retrieve the correct response from this datastack. Thanks to the ruthless precision of his android brain, the pilot can simulate billions of possible strategies in the span of a few nanoseconds.

Doom Scythes are often deployed to sap the resolve of the enemy before the battle proper begins, for their presence induces an almost irrational terror in living creatures. The Doom Scythe's primary propulsion system is a scaled up and augmented version of the dimensional repulsor drive employed on Tomb Blades. On those smaller craft, the whine of the drive is piercing and discomforting. On a Doom Scythe, the scale and amplitude of the sound is many hundreds of times greater; it resonates deep within the primitive core of living brains, playing havoc with memory, perception and sanity. Victims collapse into catatonia, slump into slack-jawed vacuity and suffer hallucinations of their dead comrades returned to worm-eaten life. Little wonder is it then that entire armies of battle-tested veterans have been known to throw down their weapons and flee at a Doom Scythe's onset, or else gouge out their own eyes in futile attempts to stem the images scratching at their senses. The distinctive crescent shape of this fighter craft has come to be associated with imminent catastrophe on a hundred different worlds, for the terror it induces lingers within the mind, carried to the grave by those who have experienced it.

Should the foe not yield the battle on the Doom Scythe's first pass, its pilot will then unleash the full fury of his craft's firepower. Tesla destructors explode into life, raking the battlefield with arcs of eldritch lightning, instantly incinerating any infantry not cowering in cover. Armoured targets can perhaps weather this sizzling storm, but they cannot hope to stand against the fury of the Doom Scythe's main weapon – the aptly named and rightly feared death ray.

There is seldom a warning before the death ray strikes, for any sound it makes is lost under the unearthly wailing of the Doom Scythe's engines. A particularly alert foe might recognise the nimbus of energy building up around the craft's focusing crystal, or the abrupt change in air pressure, but few recognise the significance quickly enough. The nimbus pulses one final time and an irresistible beam of blinding white light bursts from the Doom Scythe's underside, vaporising infantry and tanks alike, leaving only charred and rutted terrain in its wake. A single Doom Scythe can carve its way through an entire armoured column so long as its death ray remains operational, and a full squadron can reduce the sprawling spires of a hive city to fulminating slag in less than an hour.

# DOOMSDAY ARKS

All Overlords hold an absolute belief in victory through overwhelming firepower. Some of the dynasties' bitterest enemies have claimed this is simply due to the Necrons' android forms being somewhat less than dextrous, and hence ill suited to close-quarters combat. However, the truth of the matter is that, as flesh and as machine, the Necrons have always won their wars through the unrelenting application of superior technology. As such victories are invariably won at a distance, all Necron battle codices emphasise ranged superiority. Nowhere is this more evident than in the Doomsday Ark, amongst the most feared of all weapons in the Necron arsenal.

In aspect, the Doomsday Ark appears deceptively fragile; its structure is skeletal and lacks the armour plates of more conventional battle vehicles. But to obsess on this apparent fragility is to overlook the Doomsday Ark's true purpose and potential. It is not a battle tank, intended to sit in the midst of a battle line, to give and receive punishing blows. Rather, the Doomsday Ark is nothing less than an enormous self-propelled doomsday cannon – a weapon that can win a battle with but a single shot. Any systems not directly pertaining to the Doomsday Ark's main armament are part of the motive units that propel it into position, or the shielding arrays that give it some measure of protection from enemy fire. Each of these secondary systems draws power from the same source as the doomsday cannon. When deploying defensively, the legions of the Nihilakh Dynasty leave their Doomsday Arks stationary at all times to optimise their power unless there is no other choice.

The doomsday cannon itself is a wonder of super-technology, easily eclipsing the primitive energy weapons of the Imperium. Even fired at low power the doomsday cannon is a fearsome weapon; when firing at full effect, its searing energy beams burn many times hotter than more conventional plasma weapons. Infantry caught in the doomsday cannon's fury are obliterated instantly, and even heavily armoured vehicles are brought low by its high-powered beam. In the face of a doomsday cannon, nothing less than a Titan's void shields offer anything more than a fool's hope of protection.

Unlike other vehicles, the Doomsday Ark relies little on either evasion or resilience for survival. Rather, its pilot's entire defensive strategy is one of pre-emptive strike – after all, enemies are infinitely less threatening once reduced to an expanding cloud of superheated energy. Thus does anything less than an overwhelming frontal assault on a Doomsday Ark inevitably end in disaster, the attackers vaporised long before their own weapons come into range. Nor do attempts to outflank serve any better. Though ponderous in advancing, the Doomsday Ark can be brought around to a new heading with surprising speed, emerald energy beams lancing out to slaughter its would-be destroyers.

> 'There is a simple pleasure to be found in watching the enemy's crude war machines desperately attempt to evade the killing beam of a doomsday cannon, knowing their efforts are futile and they have mere moments to live.'
>
> - Cryptek Fahrza

# MONOLITHS

Nothing is so emblematic of Necron implacability as the Monolith. Like all Necron constructs, it is composed of living metal – a complex semi-sentient alloy that ripples and flows to repair damage in a blink of an eye. Target matrices and motive units, power conduits and command nodes – all are capable of comprehensive and near-instantaneous self repair. When combined with the vehicle's slab-sided armour plates, this makes the Monolith an incredibly daunting opponent for any enemy. Energy beams are absorbed and dispersed, whilst tank-busting missiles simply ricochet off the Monolith's armoured hide, leaving behind minor damage that is swiftly repaired by the living metal's arcane function.

The only way to truly halt the advance of a Monolith is to target it with a sustained period of focused fire. Only by punching through the armoured shell to the vital systems and crew within can there be any hope of ending its threat. Few enemies, however, have the discipline to be so precise under battlefield conditions, and even they must be swift in their targeting, lest they be disintegrated by the Monolith's formidable array of weaponry.

Even a single Monolith can muster enough firepower to neutralise a small army in its own right. Most dramatic of its armaments is the particle whip, channelled through a glowing focus crystal atop the vehicle. A single ear-splitting discharge from the particle whip is enough to debilitate tanks and reduce infantry to molecular vapour. Any enemies lucky enough to have survived will then have to run the gauntlet of the Monolith's gauss flux arcs. Mounted on the corners of the Monolith's upper layers, these automated defence arrays rake the area around the Monolith in pre-programmed execution patterns, finely tuned to predict the panicked motions of foes under fire.

Yet the Monolith's most fearsome weapon is its eternity gate, a system so advanced it makes a particle whip seem primitive by comparison. Originally invented by the Nephrekh, this shimmering energy field is nothing less than a captive wormhole, bound into the very heart of the Monolith. With a simple mental command, the Monolith's crew can transform the eternity gate into a portal of exile, and those that fail to resist its pull are sucked out of reality entirely, banished forever to a temporal prison from which there can be no escape. Alternatively, the Monolith's crew can use the eternity gate as a form of dimensional corridor, pulling squads of Necrons from elsewhere on the battlefield, orbiting starships or even far-distant tomb worlds and deploying them to the Monolith's location. So is the Monolith rightly known as a forerunner to disaster, for where a Monolith teleports onto a planet's surface, an invading Necron army is rarely far behind…

# OBELISKS

Obelisks are guardian-class war machines, similar in design to Monoliths but wholly different in function and purpose. Seeded throughout a tomb world's cities, their task is to lie in wait for the day when a lesser race chances its arm against a Necron world. Should that hour come, the Obelisks will rise as one from the sands to form a grid of floating bastions, all but impervious to enemy weaponry as they crush earthbound invaders with pulses of dense energy and pluck airborne targets from the skies with invisible waves that tear passing aircraft apart.

Obelisks are almost undetectable whilst dormant, a fact that has led to more than one distinctly unpleasant surprise for the invaders of a tomb world. They can be sustained for thousands, even millions, of years on the merest trickle of power, an energy emission far beneath the scryings of the younger races. Only when the Obelisks detect enemy craft in the skies above their tomb do they wake to full function. Manipulating the planet's gravity, they rise gracefully into the air, their approach swift but silent and their hulls protected by internalised energy fields. Before even a

single landing craft can touch the surface, the web of Obelisks is complete – a sentient atmospheric minefield whose operational matrix swiftly shifts to aggression protocols in reaction to approaching threats.

Should an enemy aircraft or skimmer stray too close, the Obelisk triggers a grav-pulse, an expanding sphere of force that sends the intruder spinning out of control even as it shorts out their systems. Assuming the vessel does not simply shatter on impact, the next few moments are filled with desperation for its stricken pilot. If they are sufficiently skilled and fortunate, they

might regain enough control over their craft to remain aloft – only to be met by a barrage of fire from the Obelisk's tesla spheres. Most aircraft never recover from the invisible attack of one of these massive gravity engines, let alone the sustained salvo of crackling tesla energy that follows it. Fighter squadrons and bomber waves are hurled into unrecoverable dives that end with their flaming wreckage strewn across the landscape.

When the skies are clear and the ground war still rages, the Obelisk will descend with stately grace to hover close to the planet's surface. There it forms a kind of mobile artillery piece, lending support to the phalanxes that march in its shadow. Upon detecting the presence of unfamiliar life forms or war machines, its gravitic pulses flatten the meagre intruders whilst its tesla energies blast apart anything that it still recognises as a threat. Thus awakened, the Obelisk will then form a mobile defence base for its dynasty's phalanxes from that point onwards, its living metal bulk and Canoptek repair systems making it an inviolable anchor around which hinges the greater Necron assault.

# TESSERACT VAULTS

Tesseract Vaults are mobile containment engines that crackle with killing power. They have more in common with the pyramidal buildings of a tomb complex than with conventional war machines. The creature held captive within this thrumming, floating marvel of techno-arcana is a C'tan Shard of surpassing potency.

Not all C'tan Shards are equal in size and power. Some are mere fragments of energy, scarcely powerful enough to hold themselves together. Such fractured essences are of little threat to other creatures, and of no use as weapons – if they serve any function at all, it is as curios or trinkets for acquisitive Crypteks. On the other end of that scale are the Transcendent Shards – C'tan remnants of such size that even the most reckless of Overlords think carefully before employing them. These beings are sometimes created through several shards of the same C'tan flowing into one another to become an echo of its former godlike power. The most potent of these beings are beyond the control of ordinary shackles, and are too powerful to be contained within the metaphysical folds of a Tesseract Labyrinth. If they are to serve the Necron cause at all, they must do so from the hearts of monolithic Tesseract Vaults. Trapped within the polychronon sections of the vault, the C'tan's star-born aura powers the deadly machine, but also disintegrates it at the same time, for the energies of a captive star-predator erode and break apart even the living metals of the Necrons. The Tesseract Vault therefore teems with attendant scarabs, Canoptek constructs that constantly rebuild the vault even as it comes apart.

A Tesseract Vault serves as both prison and conduit for a Transcendent C'tan Shard. Its hull contains layers of hyper-advanced node matrices and a brace of Canoptek leeches, creatures designed to redirect a portion of the shard's energies into the very cage that holds it captive. Thus, the more powerful the shard, the stronger are the chains that bind it. Hovering above the shard is a Canoptek sentinel, a many-armed construct possessed of incredible durability due to the impervium hyperalloys of its construction. The Canoptek sentinel is the only creature with molecular strength enough to survive such close proximity to a Transcendent C'tan; this gaoler-creature exists only to marshal the intense aura of power exuding from the vault's captive, and keeps it subservient to its Necron masters.

Even with a measure of their being given over to their own containment, Transcendent Shards are foes almost beyond parallel. Unlike the lesser shards, they are keenly aware of the might and glory that once lay at their command, and with that knowledge comes unbridled power and malevolence. The C'tan of old were much given to whimsical displays of destruction, and a Transcendent Shard's only solace in capture is bringing suffering and death wherever it may. With but a gesture, it sends waves of entropy gusting across the battlefield, aging foes to dust. A single spark loosed from its eyes sets cities ablaze, or triggers seismic shifts in the planetary crust. All this it does at the command of its Necron masters – at least whilst the Tesseract Vault remains intact. Should its prison's systems fail, however, the C'tan slave within will waste little time in exacting vengeance upon its erstwhile masters before vanishing into a dimensional refuge to regenerate.

# CANOPTEK WRAITHS

While a tomb world fitfully slumbers, Canoptek Wraiths are its eyes and ears. They flit silently through the dusty halls, patrolling for intruders and inspecting systems for damage and decay. The Wraiths are primarily probe mechanoids, programmed to report back to their Canoptek Spyder controllers via interstitial interface, rather than to act under their own cognisance. When orders are received, the Wraith carries them out with unfaltering resolve. Be it commanded to strike against an intruder, or conduct repairs in the heart of a collapsing tomb, the Wraith will follow instructions to completion, or die trying to do so.

The Canoptek Wraith's most notable feature is its dimensional destabilisation matrix – a phase shifter that allows it to skip in and out of reality. It can even adjust the modulation of the matrix in order to keep sections of its form in different states. Whilst a completely phased-out existence can be sustained almost indefinitely, a half-phased state takes a great deal of energy to sustain. Indeed, the Wraith's body is little more than a series of interlocking power generators and etherium lode conduits, and even so it can exist in dual states for only limited periods of time.

The dimensional destabilisation matrix was originally conceived to allow the Wraiths to reach into and repair solid machinery without all the trouble of removing outer components or armoured casings. It is, however, no less valuable when dealing with intruders – if the timing is correct, a Canoptek Wraith can phase its claws and tendrils inside an opponent, swiftly resolidifying them to sever arteries, nerve clusters and other vital pathways without leaving an external mark to show for it. Furthermore, the foe must time their return blows with care, lest their weapons pass through the Wraith's phased-out form.

Though their primary function is to watch over their sleeping masters, Wraiths are often drafted into armies to serve as advance scouts. The dimensional destabilisation matrix allows a Wraith to traverse all manner of terrain without pause and also serves to hide it from enemy eyes and sensors. Many an enemy army has advanced across a tomb world, little knowing that its every move is watched, recorded and reported on by the ghostly Canoptek Wraith. Only the most observant of foes can hope to catch sight of the lurking Wraith's spectral form or detect the unsettling electronic chatter that accompanies its precise transmissions. Even then, such things are commonly dismissed as tricks of the imagination.

Once the inevitable battle begins, the Canoptek Wraith is then tasked with sowing terror and disorder throughout the enemy ranks by striking at commanders, support troops and supply lines – anything that a more conventional strike force would struggle to reach. Indeed, sometimes an enemy commander won't even make it to the battle. Instead they are slain in their sleep the night before by the cold claws of a Canoptek Wraith assassin to whom doors, guards and force fields are no barrier.

# CANOPTEK SPYDERS

Unlike their Necron masters, Canoptek Spyders never sleep, but wile away the aeons servicing the structures of their tomb world. Even in their prime, these systems required constantly looped maintenance cycles lest they degraded beyond repair, and the withering centuries have only hastened this natural decay. It is a task both endless in scope and thankless in nature, but Canoptek Spyders are patient unto eternity.

Though it is essentially just an automated drone, a Canoptek Spyder is still a formidable foe when the situation demands. Its vast arrays of self-repair and backup systems, vital for enduring the uncaring millennia, offer substantial protection against a foe's weaponry. In return, any enemy foolish enough to stray within reach of the Canoptek Spyder will have flesh scoured from bone by an array of mechanical tools and pincers. As if this were not enough, each Canoptek Spyder will have a further selection of weaponry at its command, depending upon its function. Canoptek Spyders whose primary duties are oversight, rather than direct action, craft slaved hosts of Canoptek Scarabs and nanoscarabs within their abdomens, which are unleashed to effect repairs on nearby Necrons, or consume enemy weapons and armour. Others employ particle beam dissectors and act as sentinels for the slumbering tomb.

Whilst Canoptek Spyders are not sentient by any strict definition, their complex and layered subroutines are incredibly resilient and can adapt to most situations. If a triad of Canoptek Spyders are operating in concert, one takes overall command, harnessing the processing capacity of the others to create a gestalt supermind far greater than the sum of its parts. This hyper-efficiency is passed on to all Canoptek Wraiths and Canoptek Scarabs in the immediate vicinity, allowing the Canoptek Spyders to affect a coordinated and precise response to any threat, be it a failed stasis-matrix or an enemy incursion. So it is that any intruders to a tomb are often slain before catching so much as a glimpse of a Necron, having already been overwhelmed by swarms of Scarabs and Wraiths silently directed by a looming Canoptek Spyder and ensuring the safety of their slumbering masters.

*Entry 13.6.214 – We held them off until dawn, blasting away with the last of our las rounds. Domor fell hard. The swarm stripped the flesh from his bones in moments. We cannot last another day. A thousand miles of ice stand between us and Delta Fortitude, but we cannot stay here. Tonight they will come again.*

*Entry 13.6.217 – Our fuel runs low. I cannot feel my hands. When I look at them I see raw blue flesh. Throne of the Emperor, it is so cold. But rather this death than what awaited us in the depths of Excavation 43 Vertigrade.*

*Entry 31.6.220 – God-Emperor, they are here. They have taken them all. I am the last. I feel their gaze upon me, a constellation of pitiless azure eyes. I see their scorpid forms, skittering through the darkness. Ever closer. Why do they not come for me too? God-Emperor of Terra, why do they not just kill me?*

*- Recovered from the journal of Cpt Corvin Prassus, 5th Terventia Engineers*

# CANOPTEK SCARABS

Canoptek Scarabs are constructs, designed to break down organic and non-organic matter into raw energy. This harvested energy can then be woven into fresh forms at the direction of the Scarabs' controller. In the confines of a tomb, this invariably involves stripping down destroyed or damaged components which can then be reborn as replacement parts, or else as further Canoptek Spyders, Scarabs or Wraiths to oversee and manage the tomb's functions. Almost anything can be replicated in this fashion, providing that the wellspring of energy is sufficient to the task at hand. Given time, a suitably large swarm of Scarabs can consume an entire hive city and all its inhabitants, thereafter using the purloined energies to create anything from a battlefleet to a fully functioning Necron tomb ready for habitation.

With their swift, darting movements and high-pitched chittering, Canoptek Scarabs appear to mimic the behaviours of organic invertebrates. However, they lack for a true hive mind. A swarm of Scarabs has no more intelligence than one Scarab alone – which is to say none at all – and is driven by simple instructions and even simpler instincts.

Essentially mindless feeding machines, Canoptek Scarabs are typically controlled by interstitial carrier waves from Canoptek Spyders or Crypteks. If this signal is disrupted or jammed, Canoptek Scarabs simply revert to their most basic instincts and devour anything in the immediate vicinity – even other Scarabs or Necrons. However, the interstitial interfaces are incredibly difficult to detect, let alone disrupt. Should the controlling entity be

destroyed, another automatically assumes control within moments. Even if the enemy can completely remove the carrier waves, this often creates a far greater problem than before. The Canoptek Scarabs will no longer operate under the Necrons' direct control, and as part of their reversion to base programming they will expend any accumulated energy on fashioning ever more Scarabs, thus creating a voracious self-replicating swarm that only something of the order of saturation bombardment has any hope of exterminating.

An Overlord will often begin a battle by unleashing a swarm of Canoptek Scarabs, hoping that the foe will waste much-needed ammunition blasting the scavengers apart before the true assault is launched. Hardened troops may be able to destroy or drive off the Scarabs with disciplined volleys, whereas other enemies will be driven mad with fear by the pervasive drone of the swarm's wings, or even overwhelmed and devoured by the chittering tide. Either way, an observant Overlord can glean valuable information as to where the strongest pockets of resistance lie and plan his attacks accordingly.

However, where Canoptek Scarabs truly come into their own is when unleashed upon tanks and other vehicles. Once a Scarab has latched onto a hull, it begins to feed, breaking down the victim's armour plating and leaving it vulnerable to attacks from other sources. If not quickly destroyed or driven away, a swarm of Canoptek Scarabs can even burrow their way through the hull, turning a mighty engine of war into a horror-filled prison for its soon-to-be devoured crew.

> 'Take my advice: if you hear the chittering of Scarab wings, just run, and keep running 'til the sound is gone. Don't stop, and don't look back. If one of your squad-mates starts screaming, it's because the Scarabs are on him, and you'll die right alongside if you try to help.'
>
> - Quartermaster Kross, Cadian 312th, executed for dishonourable conduct 777.M41

# C'TAN SHARDS

C'tan Shards are all that remain of the once mighty star gods. They are echoes of their former selves, splinters of energy that survived the Necrons' betrayal and were enslaved in turn. Most now languish in unbreakable servitude to their former vassals, utterly incapable of acting without commission. Should a C'tan Shard rebel, or a fault develop in its control relays, then fail-safe mechanisms automatically activate, whisking the creature back to its tomb, there to languish for centuries until times are dire enough that its services must be called upon again. Even with these precautions, the Necrons are wary of employing C'tan Shards in battle. Though the chance of escape is remote, the possibility remains, so the day must be dark indeed before the tesseract labyrinths are opened and the C'tan unleashed upon the galaxy.

Despite their reduced and wholly fettered state, C'tan Shards are still beings of near-unlimited power. They can manifest energy blasts, control the minds of lesser beings, manipulate the flow of time, and banish foes to alternate realities. Indeed, a C'tan Shard's abilities are limited only by two things: its imagination – which is immense – and glimmering memories of the being from which it was severed. Whilst no individual C'tan Shard has full recall of the omnipotent creature it once was, each carries the personality and hubris of that far vaster and more puissant being. Though a C'tan Shard has the power to reduce a tank to molten slag with but a gesture, it might simply not occur to it to do so, as its gestalt primogenitor would have tackled the situation through other means, such as by devolving the crew into primordial ooze, or deceiving them into attacking their own allies. The only hope of defeating a C'tan is to breach its necrodermis – the hyperphysical skin of living metal that cages its essence. If the necrodermis is compromised, the C'tan Shard explodes in a pulse of blinding energy, its being scattered to the galactic winds.

Even the Transcendent C'tan, mightiest of their kind, can be loosed from their prison vaults if the situation is grave enough to require it, though the potential ramifications are dire – the longer these wilful beings spend outside their prisons, the more clearly the fractured memories of their past begin to manifest, and the more rapidly the Necrons' hold over them begins to degrade.

Whilst it is true that many C'tan Shards are now indentured to Necron service, this by no means accounts for the entire pantheon. Discrepant information from varied and varyingly reliable sources causes great confusion concerning the exact number and nature of the surviving C'tan, even among the Aeldari. Records held in the Black Library contradict those maintained on Ulthwé, which are again at odds with the archives held on Alaitoc. Some claim there exists a slumbering star god deep beneath the canyons of the red planet Mars, others that the ravenous C'tan known as the Outsider was tricked by Cegorach into eating its own brothers, and now dwells in exile within a hollow planet far to the galactic south. However, all Aeldari agree that the splinters of knowledge held by the Imperium are flawed and confused. The Adeptus Mechanicus scholars who covet the ancient lore of the C'tan are as likely to pass over possible revelation as they are to move further from the truth with each fresh discovery made. Any soul of sufficient learning or determination who goes looking for proof of a C'tan's existence can eventually uncover it, but this speaks more to the mindset of the seeker than it does to any value of the 'evidence'.

'They came to us as gods and we, like fools, took them at their word. Mephet'ran the Deceiver, Aza'gorod the Nightbringer, Iash'uddra the Endless Swarm – I curse their names, and the names of all their malevolent brethren.'

*- From the Chronicle of Szarekh, Last of the Silent Kings*

# THE NIGHTBRINGER

The Nightbringer was once death incarnate, a sadistic god with the power to unmake the stars. It delighted in inflicting pain and suffering not only to feed, but simply because it could. Its gaze was death and its mighty scythe feasted on the annihilation of civilisations. In ages long past, the Nightbringer destroyed entire star systems on a whim, gorging itself on the agonies of countless billions of ended lives. Now, however, it is bound as little more than shards of its former majesty.

With the biotransference of the Necrontyr, much of what was known about the star gods faded into mythology. Awareness of the Nightbringer, however, has remained with every race since that time. The war between the Old Ones and the C'tan unleashed forces beyond understanding, and the suffering caused among the elder races was beyond reckoning. Of all the star gods, the Nightbringer inflicted the greatest misery upon the galaxy. So profound was this legacy that fear of its silhouette is still felt keenly by a million species.

The very star under which the Necrontyr race lived their brief, morbid lives gave birth to the vast sun-spanning energy that was the Nightbringer. In their quest for a weapon with which to defeat the Old Ones, the Necrontyr turned to the mighty coalescent energy feeding within the photosphere of their star. The first of the C'tan to manifest openly, the Nightbringer brought with it the kiss of death that had plagued the Necrontyr race since their birth. Having fed on the sustaining but flavourless power of a star, the Nightbringer found the epicurean delights of the Necrontyr's awe and fear much more to its liking. It slaughtered those who dared address it directly, feeding on the essence of their terror and suffering. Its appetite knew no bounds, and only with desperate pledges of servitude were the Necrontyr able to convince the creature that there were more races beyond their world that could be feasted upon – sentient beings beyond number for it to destroy.

Soon after, the Necrontyr awoke the powers of many more star gods, for a time becoming their willing servants in the war against the Old Ones. Like the other C'tan, the Nightbringer craved worshippers and slaves to satisfy its monstrous ego. Many of its servants descended into murderous insanity, unable to withstand the bloody visions their master's presence brought on. Grown strong on endless slaughter, nothing else could satisfy its hunger.

The Nightbringer eagerly threw itself into the war against the Old Ones, laying waste to entire regions of space in the name of its own monstrous appetite. As the fighting dragged on and the colossal scale of destruction grew, the Nightbringer became increasingly detached from the cause it had supposedly been fighting for, content merely to destroy and feed at will. Even when the Old Ones were defeated and scoured from the galaxy, the Nightbringer fought on against all living things. It used its powers to reach into the minds of the young races and plant the seeds of their darkest fears, nurturing whole species whose entire existence was suffused with the horror of death and mortality. Ultimately, the Nightbringer was undone when its rival the Deceiver convinced it that the most succulent feasts were to be had in the living energies of its fellow C'tan. So began a reign of murder as the Nightbringer brought all its powers to bear in hunting down its fellow gods.

Had it not been glutted to the point of hubris on the essences of its fellow star gods, the Nightbringer might not have fallen. After the last of the Old Ones were banished, the C'tan was brought low by those it thought beneath its notice. Its essence was shattered by god-killing hypercannons devised by the finest Crypteks in the galaxy – weapons the Nightbringer was convinced were built out of tribute, but which were turned upon it as it feasted. It was bound within an array of necrodermis containment units and trammelled under the rule of those it once called slaves.

By the time the Necrontyr finally brought the Nightbringer down, primordial fear of this star-killing monstrosity had already been imprinted upon the collective psyche of many more races than it could ever have fed upon. It had become the personification of death in every species' racial memory, and even though the Necrons that had once served it sought to use this innate fear for their own purposes, the terror of mortality was the Nightbringer's parting gift to the galaxy. To the Aeldari it was known as *Kaelis Ra*, the Destroyer of Light, while to the emergent race of Mankind, it simply became the Reaper. Of all the young races, only the Krork escaped the Nightbringer's boon; the race that would one day become the Orks were thus spared the fear of death.

Though the Nightbringer's power has been broken, the shards that remain are still the most powerful of their kind. All fear the Reaper, for it casts a long shadow indeed.

> 'Aza'gorod, the Nightbringer. The embodiment of death. A killer of stars, and of worlds. An eater of gods. The Old Ones themselves could not stand before this star-spawned creature.
>
> And yet, as shall be the fate of all things, the Nightbringer was broken beneath the heel of the Necron Empire, bound and humbled. If such a creature can be leashed to our will, then there is nothing that we cannot accomplish. Never again will we bow to any master. Never again shall we cede command of our destiny.'
>
> – Illuminor Szeras

# THE DECEIVER

The Deceiver's greatest achievements are wrought from deception and lies. Subtle and charming, its web of half-truths and outrageous falsehoods have led planets to their doom and great leaders into slavery. Even when the Necrontyr were still clothed in flesh, the other C'tan learned to shun the influence of the Deceiver, for it was duplicity itself.

Of all the so-called star gods, the one known as the Deceiver was the most insidious and capricious. The little that can be gleaned indicates that even the Necrontyr knew few truths about this entity when they first encountered it. Its manifestation was a time of great rejoicing among the Necrontyr – they were awe-struck by its fluid transition to an earthly form among them, and the ease with which it adapted to the realm of matter. They first named it *Mephet'ran*, the Messenger, and believed it was a bridge to mediate between themselves and the other star gods.

As the C'tan began to gather followers and devotees, the being known as the Messenger soon outstripped its peers in influence. The star gods seemed too remote and awe-inspiring for many Necrontyr, but Mephet'ran communed in ways they understood. Perhaps this was because it was never as powerful as the other C'tan, and used guile and skill to secure its future. With its mortal puppets dancing to its tune, the messenger stoked the fires of hatred that the Necrontyr felt towards the Old Ones. In doing so it drew them towards a war which would burn the galaxy to cinders.

It was the Deceiver that orchestrated the process of biotransference throughout the Necrontyr race – not suggesting it outright, but planting the seeds in the minds of others so they eventually suggested it themselves. In time, the C'tan offered the Necrontyr their great and deadly gift. The short-lived race, ever blighted by their uncertain existence, gained immortality, but at a terrible price. By giving themselves to the star gods utterly, the Necrontyr were consumed and remade, their minds embedded into machines of living metal so they might fight on forever more.

Despite the Messenger's godly charisma and unbound skill in the art of subterfuge, there were a few amongst the Necrontyr – Orikan the Diviner amongst them – that were riven with doubt as to its intentions. Those who had not surrendered to the gods already were enjoined by the rest to submit, but could not

be persuaded to make such a giant leap of faith. It was only then that the Deceiver's true face began to show as it lured the unbelievers into the clutches of the faithful with promises of mediation and compromise. All bar Orikan himself were seized by the Deceiver's followers and delivered to their fate, whether willingly or not. Then the believers themselves were added to the glittering ranks of unliving machines. Eventually the Necrontyr race was utterly purged, becoming instead the Necrons, cursed to eternal servitude.

The War in Heaven escalated time and time again, with the C'tan at the heart of each new engagement, and their silvered legions at their side. In many ways the doubt and mistrust sowed between the young races by the Deceiver contributed more to the star gods' cause than any number of legions or ships. Yet even when its foes lay scattered and slain, the Deceiver could not help but sow discord to amuse itself. As the C'tan gained ascendancy over the Old Ones and the harvests of sentient populations grew thin, it was the Deceiver who first set one C'tan against another.

Driven at first by bravado and later by desperation, the C'tan fought their personal wars with a casual disregard for their slave races, leaving millions dead and whole star systems consumed. In a whirl of pacts and betrayals the Deceiver tricked and consumed several of its fellows, but it still remained the weakest of the C'tan in terms of raw power, and was always careful to avoid the clutches of the mightiest. Aeldari legends portray a figure they refer to as the Jackal God as helping and hindering both sides equally, always keeping itself at the edges of a conflict where it could take advantage of any opportunity or weakness.

This same deviousness proved to be the Deceiver's undoing. Its schemes were close to perfect, but absolute perfection eluded it. Ultimately word spread of its manipulations, and its reputation became tarnished, then torn into tatters. When the C'tan were ambushed and laid low by the slave race they had created, none came to the Deceiver's aid. He was fettered, bound and broken into shards. Now the Deceiver is the unwitting tool of the race he once enslaved. Each shard believes itself in control, fighting alongside the Necrons the better to manipulate them. In reality, it is the Deceiver that is deluded, forced by its former minions into an eternity of servitude in a cosmic irony that will never end.

'The being known as Mephet'ran came to us, speaking honeyed platitudes and half-truths, and to my shame we heeded its words. We exchanged the soul of our race for the illusion of emancipation.

My revenge, when at last it came, earned me but a sliver of satisfaction. It pleases me to know that this avatar of disruption is now slaved to the cause of Necron dominance and galactic order. I only hope that this is as torturous a fate for the Deceiver as the weight of failure is for myself.'

- Szarekh, Last of the Silent Kings

# THE IMMORTAL ARMIES

Their weapons glowing with baleful light, rank after rank of skeletal metal warriors march relentlessly towards the foe, their arrival heralding the rebirth of an empire. Resplendent in their dynastic colours and hieroglyphs, a Necron army makes for a truly impressive sight.

Imotekh the Stormlord

Nemesor Zahndrekh

Vargard Obyron

Overlord with voidscythe and resurrection orb

The Novokh march forth to sweep Imperial trespassers from their tomb world. Sickle-shaped war machines send flesh-melting beams of energy arcing through the ranks of the Salamanders, while rank after rank of Necron Warriors advance with weapons blazing.

These Lychguard serve the masters of the Sautekh Dynasty as implacable guardians. Two wield hyperphase swords and dispersion shields, while one carries a warscythe.

Necron Warriors and Immortals often bear a phalanx glyph upon their back.

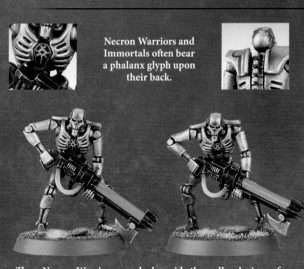

These Necron Warriors march alongside the endless legions of the Sautekh Dynasty, slaying the foes of the Empire with their gauss flayers. They bear the dynastic glyph on the centre of their metal skeleton.

Sautekh Dynasty Triarch Praetorian armed with a rod of covenant

For millennia these Immortals have marched and killed in the name of the Sautekh Dynasty. Two of these battle-hardened veterans wield gauss blasters, while the other carries a tesla carbine.

When the rulers of the Sautekh Dynasty seek the death of a particular foe, they dispatch these Deathmarks, sniper-assassins who wield synaptic disintegrators; a single shot from these rifles obliterates the neural tissue of their target.

**Novokh Dynasty Immortal with tesla carbine**

**Thokt Dynasty Warrior with gauss flayer**

**Nephrekh Dynasty Warrior with gauss flayer**

**Nephrekh Dynasty Immortal with gauss blaster**

**Immortal with tesla carbine**

**Nekthyst Dynasty Immortal with gauss blaster**

**Ogdobekh Dynasty Lychguard with hyperphase sword and dispersion shield**

**Flayed One**

**Deathmark from the Sekemtar Dynasty**

C'tan Shard of the Deceiver

C'tan Shard of the Nightbringer

Overlord with staff of light and resurrection orb

Catacomb Command Barge with gauss cannon

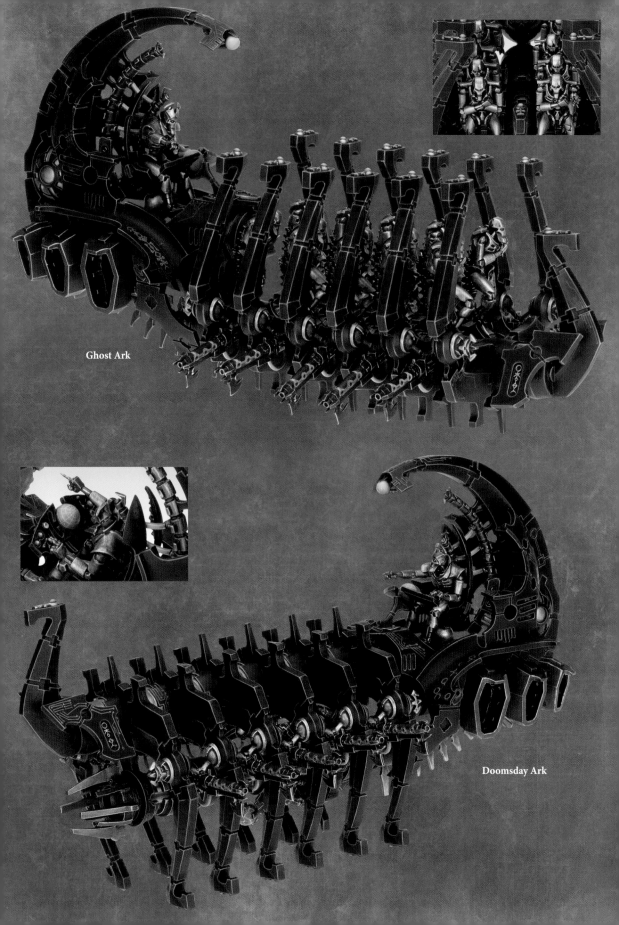

Ghost Ark

Doomsday Ark

The blood-red markings of the Novokh are a warning of the appalling carnage to come when this warlike dynasty takes to the battlefield. The Novokh's fearsome warriors become invigorated with every fresh kill, the sight of spurting gore reigniting long-lost memories of conquest.

The Nihilakh bedeck their warriors and war machines in gold and royal aquamarine, displaying their great wealth and regal glory for all to see. The awe-inspiring sight of the dynasty's arrayed legions is magnified a hundredfold when they take to the battlefield.

An assembled Mephrit army glows brightly with the light of harnessed suns, every warrior of the dynasty carrying a weapon imbued with formidable solar energy. When unleashed, the accumulated flare of these instruments of death is blinding in its intensity.

Where Imotekh the Stormlord leads his armies, the galaxy cowers before his unquestioned might. His legions contain some of the most brilliant strategists and warriors in the Necron Empire, such as the redoubtable champion known as Vargard Obyron.

Cryptek with staff of light and Canoptek cloak

Orikan the Diviner

Illuminor Szeras

# AWAKENING THE LEGIONS

A Necron army is a resilient and deadly wall of living metal, able to devastate the enemy with a fearsome arsenal of ranged and close-combat weapons while shrugging off a truly impressive amount of firepower. The sample armies displayed below illustrate this faction's unique strengths in two very different ways.

The first sample collection is designed to dominate in close combat, while enduring and repairing any damage the opposing enemy can inflict. A squad of Immortals armed with gauss blasters provides a solid base of fire, while three Canoptek Wraiths skim speedily towards the foe to tear at them with their gleaming claws. The formation is led by a Cryptek, whose Technomancer ability improves the reanimation protocols of nearby units. Finally, a unit of Lychguard provides a defensive shield around the Cryptek. This Battle-forged force contains an HQ choice, a Troops choice, an Elites choice and a Fast Attack choice. It therefore qualifies as a Patrol Detachment, detailed in the *Warhammer 40,000* rulebook, providing three Command Points to spend on Stratagems.

The second army is based around the Start Collecting! Necrons box, and is led by a Necron Overlord. It contains a unit of Lychguard, a unit of Necron Warriors and a unit of Immortals. This strong core of infantry is supported by an Annihilation Barge and a towering Triarch Stalker, as well as a single unit of both Flayed Ones and Canoptek Scarabs. As it includes three Elites choices, this collection qualifies as a Vanguard Detachment, earning an extra Command Point in addition to the three granted for being a Battle-forged army, for a total of four Command Points.

This is a relatively small starting force that can nonetheless inflict serious damage on its enemies while being remarkably durable.

This is a well-balanced and effective force, possessing a variety of weapons and abilities that will allow it to deal with any opposition.

# THE SCYTHE OF ZABAREAS

**The proud Necron Overlord known as Zabareas the All-Seeing leads his soulless legions from their dank crypts and out into the stars, in search of conquest and glory. By his will shall the lesser races of the galaxy be humbled and their armies broken.**

Zabareas the All-Seeing marches at the head of his battle-hardened army, guarded by an elite retinue of Lychguard known as the Unbroken. While the Overlord directs the battle and drives his soulless warriors on to victory with incisive strategy and the sheer power of his presence, these elite guards contemptuously dispose of any foes foolish enough to stray close.

Three units of Necron Warriors form the backbone of Zabareas' conquering force, passionless automatons who absorb the majority of the enemy's fire. Zabareas often assigns a Ghost Ark to transport them swiftly to the most fiercely contested areas of the battlefield. Three units of Immortals, veterans of countless campaigns, provide

overwhelming fire support. While this formidable wall of infantry advances relentlessly, Canoptek Scarabs skitter ahead of the line, leaping upon enemy tanks and soldiers alike and dismantling them with their razor-sharp mandibles. These small but lethal machines – along with the rest of Zabareas' Canoptek war engines – are commanded by the Cryptek Faros, a demented scientist who loves nothing more than unleashing his cybernetic menageries upon living subjects. His favoured instruments of torment are the three Canoptek Wraiths he calls the Whispering Death.

A unit of Tomb Blades skirts the edge of Zabareas' formation, ready to respond swiftly and mercilessly to any attempts by the

enemy to outflank or outmanoeuvre the Overlord's force. Such foolishness also draws the attention of Overlord Nakhmas, a kinsman of Zabareas who has been granted command of the legion's heavy armour. Overseeing the devastation from his Catacomb Command Barge, Nakhmas directs the fearsome power of a Doomsday Ark, an Annihilation Barge and a monstrous Monolith, which doubles as a dimensional gateway for Zabareas' warriors. The All-Seeing has also requested the services of a unit of Triarch Praetorians and a Triarch Stalker, who are present to keep an eye on the ambitious Nakhmas as much as they are to obliterate the foe.

This grand army fulfils the requirements of a Brigade Detachment as detailed in the *Warhammer 40,000* rulebook, and therefore earns an impressive twelve Command Points! This will provide a suite of comprehensive tactical options upon the battlefield, ensuring that the owner of this collection can dominate their opponents in the

1. Necron Overlord Zabareas
2. Lychguard 'The Unbroken'
3. Necron Warriors
4. Immortals
5. Ghost Ark
6. Canoptek Scarabs
7. Cryptek Faros
8. Canoptek Wraiths 'Whispering Death'
9. Tomb Blades
10. Catacomb Command Barge (Overlord Nakhmas)
11. Annihilation Barge
12. Triarch Praetorians
13. Triarch Stalker
14. Monolith

# THE DYNASTIES ASCENDANT

This section contains all of the datasheets that you will need to fight battles with your Necrons miniatures, and the rules for all of the weapons they can wield in battle. Each datasheet includes the characteristics profiles of the unit it describes, as well as any wargear and special abilities it may have. Any abilities that are common to several units are described below and referenced on the datasheets themselves.

## KEYWORDS

Throughout this section you will come across a keyword that is within angular brackets, specifically **<DYNASTY>**. This is shorthand for a keyword of your own choosing, as described below.

## <DYNASTY>

Most Necrons belong to a dynasty. Some datasheets specify what dynasty a Necron unit is drawn from (e.g. Imotekh the Stormlord is from the Sautekh Dynasty, and so has the **SAUTEKH** keyword). If a Necron datasheet has the **<DYNASTY>** keyword, you must nominate which dynasty that unit is from. There are many different dynasties to choose from; you can use any of the dynasties described in our books, or make up your own if you prefer. You then simply replace the **<DYNASTY>** keyword in every instance on that unit's datasheet with the name of your chosen dynasty.

For example, if you were to include a Lord in your army, and you decided it was from the Nihilakh Dynasty, then its **<DYNASTY>** keyword is changed to **NIHILAKH**, and its 'The Lord's Will' ability would say 'Re-roll wound rolls of 1 for friendly **NIHILAKH INFANTRY** units that are within 6" of this model.'

## ABILITIES

The following abilities are common to several Necron units:

### REANIMATION PROTOCOLS

*The moment a Necron is laid low, its metal body enacts complex self-repair routines, reattaching severed limbs and fusing together shattered armour plating.*

Roll a D6 for each slain model from this unit (unless the whole unit has been completely destroyed) at the beginning of your turn. Do not roll for models that have fled the unit. On a 5+, the model's reanimation protocols activate and it is returned to this unit with its full complement of wounds, otherwise it remains inactive (although you can roll again at the start of each of your subsequent turns). When a model's reanimation protocols activate, set it up in unit coherency with any model from this unit that has not returned to the unit as a result of reanimation protocols this turn, and more than 1" from enemy models. If you cannot do this because there is no room to place the model, do not set it up (you can make Reanimation Protocols rolls for this model again in subsequent turns).

### LIVING METAL

*The composite metals that comprise a Necron's skeletal form are all but impervious to destruction, and ensure that only the most grievous wounds can lay these ancient creatures low.*

At the beginning of your turn, this unit regains 1 lost wound.

# IMOTEKH THE STORMLORD

| NAME | M | WS | BS | S | T | W | A | Ld | Sv |
|---|---|---|---|---|---|---|---|---|---|
| Imotekh the Stormlord | 5" | 2+ | 2+ | 5 | 5 | 6 | 3 | 10 | 2+ |

Imotekh the Stormlord is a single model armed with the Staff of the Destroyer and a gauntlet of fire. Only one of this model may be included in your army.

| WEAPON | RANGE | TYPE | S | AP | D | ABILITIES |
|---|---|---|---|---|---|---|
| Gauntlet of fire | 8" | Assault D6 | 4 | 0 | 1 | This weapon automatically hits its target. |
| Staff of the Destroyer (shooting) | 18" | Assault 3 | 6 | -3 | 2 | - |
| Staff of the Destroyer (melee) | Melee | Melee | +1 | -3 | 2 | - |

| ABILITIES | |
|---|---|
| **Living Metal** (pg 82) | **My Will Be Done:** At the beginning your turn, choose a friendly **NECRONS INFANTRY** unit within 6" of Imotekh the Stormlord. Add 1 to Advance, charge and hit rolls for that unit until the beginning of your next turn. A unit can only be chosen as the target of this ability once in each turn. |
| **Phaeron of the Sautekh Dynasty:** Imotekh the Stormlord can use his My Will Be Done ability twice a turn, but only if you choose friendly **SAUTEKH INFANTRY** units to be affected by it both times. | |
| **Lord of the Storm:** Once per battle, in your Shooting phase, Imotekh can call the storm: pick an enemy unit within 48" of Imotekh, other than a **CHARACTER**, and roll a D6. On a 2+ that unit suffers that many mortal wounds. Then roll a D6 for each enemy unit within 6" of that unit; on a 6 the unit being rolled for suffers D3 mortal wounds. | **Bloodswarm Necroscarabs:** You can re-roll hit rolls of 1 for friendly units of **SAUTEKH** Flayed Ones that are within 12" of Imotekh the Stormlord. |
| | **Grand Strategist:** If your army is Battle-forged, you receive 1 additional Command Point if Imotekh the Stormlord is your Warlord. |
| **Undying:** Imotekh the Stormlord regains D3 lost wounds at the beginning of your turn, rather than 1, from his Living Metal ability. | **Phase Shifter:** Imotekh the Stormlord has a 4+ invulnerable save. |

| FACTION KEYWORDS | NECRONS, SAUTEKH |
|---|---|
| KEYWORDS | CHARACTER, INFANTRY, OVERLORD, IMOTEKH THE STORMLORD |

Imotekh, phaeron of the Sautekh Dynasty, is a military genius whose campaigns of terror have conquered countless star systems.

# NEMESOR ZAHNDREKH

| NAME | M | WS | BS | S | T | W | A | Ld | Sv |
|---|---|---|---|---|---|---|---|---|---|
| Nemesor Zahndrekh | 5" | 2+ | 2+ | 5 | 5 | 6 | 3 | 10 | 2+ |

Nemesor Zahndrekh is a single model armed with a staff of light. Only one of this model may be included in your army.

| WEAPON | RANGE | TYPE | S | AP | D | ABILITIES |
|---|---|---|---|---|---|---|
| Staff of light (shooting) | 12" | Assault 3 | 5 | -2 | 1 | - |
| Staff of light (melee) | Melee | Melee | User | -2 | 1 | - |

| ABILITIES | |
|---|---|
| **Living Metal** (pg 82)<br><br>**Counter Tactics:** At the beginning of your opponent's turn, choose one enemy **CHARACTER** within 12" of Nemesor Zahndrekh. Any aura abilities that character has cannot be used until the beginning of your opponent's next turn.<br><br>**Phase Shifter:** Nemesor Zahndrekh has a 4+ invulnerable save.<br><br>**My Will Be Done:** At the beginning of your turn, choose a friendly **SAUTEKH INFANTRY** unit within 6" of Nemesor Zahndrekh. Add 1 to Advance, charge and hit rolls for that unit until the beginning of your next turn. A unit can only be chosen as the target of this ability once in each turn. | **Transient Madness:** Roll a D3 at the beginning of your turn and consult the following table. Choose a friendly **SAUTEKH INFANTRY** unit within 6" of Nemesor Zahndrekh to gain the relevant ability until the beginning of your next turn.<br><br>**D3** / **Result**<br>**1** — **Avenge the Fallen:** Add 1 to the Attacks characteristic of models in this unit.<br>**2** — **Quell the Rebellion:** Improve the Ballistic Skill of models in this unit by 1 (e.g. a Ballistic Skill of 3+ becomes 2+).<br>**3** — **Solarmills? Charge!:** Re-roll failed charge rolls for this unit. |

| FACTION KEYWORDS | NECRONS, SAUTEKH |
|---|---|
| KEYWORDS | CHARACTER, INFANTRY, OVERLORD, NEMESOR ZAHNDREKH |

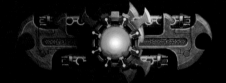

# VARGARD OBYRON

| NAME | M | WS | BS | S | T | W | A | Ld | Sv |
|---|---|---|---|---|---|---|---|---|---|
| Vargard Obyron | 5" | 2+ | 3+ | 5 | 5 | 6 | 4 | 10 | 2+ |

Vargard Obyron is a single model armed with a warscythe. Only one of this model may be included in your army.

| WEAPON | RANGE | TYPE | S | AP | D | ABILITIES |
|---|---|---|---|---|---|---|
| Warscythe | Melee | Melee | +2 | -4 | 2 | - |

| ABILITIES | |
|---|---|
| **Living Metal** (pg 82)<br><br>**Cleaving Counterblow:** If Vargard Obyron is slain during the Fight phase, do not remove his model until the end of the phase. He can still fight in this phase, if he has not already done so.<br><br>**The Lord's Will:** Re-roll wound rolls of 1 for friendly **SAUTEKH INFANTRY** units that are within 6" of Vargard Obyron. | **Ghostwalk Mantle:** At the end of any of your Movement phases, you can remove Vargard Obyron and a friendly **SAUTEKH INFANTRY** unit within 6" of Vargard Obyron (other than Nemesor Zahndrekh) from the battlefield and set them up so that all models are within 6" of Nemesor Zahndrekh and more than 1" from any enemy models.<br><br>**The Vargard's Duty:** Roll a D6 each time Nemesor Zahndrekh loses a wound whilst he is within 3" of Vargard Obyron; on a 2+ Obyron can intercept that hit – Zahndrekh does not lose a wound but Obyron suffers a mortal wound. |

| FACTION KEYWORDS | NECRONS, SAUTEKH |
|---|---|
| KEYWORDS | CHARACTER, INFANTRY, LORD, VARGARD OBYRON |

# ILLUMINOR SZERAS

| NAME | M | WS | BS | S | T | W | A | Ld | Sv |
|---|---|---|---|---|---|---|---|---|---|
| Illuminor Szeras | 6" | 3+ | 3+ | 4 | 4 | 5 | 4 | 10 | 3+ |

Illuminor Szeras is a single model armed with the Eldritch Lance. Only one of this model may be included in your army.

| WEAPON | RANGE | TYPE | S | AP | D | ABILITIES |
|---|---|---|---|---|---|---|
| Eldritch Lance (shooting) | 36" | Assault 1 | 8 | -4 | D6 | - |
| Eldritch Lance (melee) | Melee | Melee | User | -2 | 1 | - |

| ABILITIES | |
|---|---|
| **Living Metal** (pg 82) <br><br> **Master Technomancer:** Add 1 to all Reanimation Protocols rolls for models from friendly **NECRONS** units within 3" of Illuminor Szeras. A unit cannot benefit from both the Master Technomancer and Technomancer abilities in the same turn. | **Mechanical Augmentation:** At the end of your Movement phase, you can choose a friendly **NECRONS** Warriors or Immortals unit within 1" of Illuminor Szeras. Roll a D3 to see what characteristic modifier models in that unit gain for the rest of the battle: |

| D3 | Augmentation |
|---|---|
| 1 | +1 Strength |
| 2 | +1 Toughness |
| 3 | Ballistic Skill improved by 1 (e.g. a Ballistic Skill of 3+ becomes 2+) |

A unit can only be the target of this ability once per battle.

| FACTION KEYWORDS | **NECRONS** |
|---|---|
| KEYWORDS | **CHARACTER, INFANTRY, CRYPTEK, ILLUMINOR SZERAS** |

# ORIKAN THE DIVINER

| NAME | M | WS | BS | S | T | W | A | Ld | Sv |
|---|---|---|---|---|---|---|---|---|---|
| Orikan the Diviner | 5" | 3+ | 3+ | 4 | 4 | 5 | 2 | 10 | 4+ |
| Orikan Empowered | 5" | 2+ | 2+ | 7 | 7 | 7 | 4 | 10 | 4+ |

Orikan the Diviner is a single model armed with the Staff of Tomorrow. Only one of this model may be included in your army.

| WEAPON | RANGE | TYPE | S | AP | D | ABILITIES |
|---|---|---|---|---|---|---|
| Staff of Tomorrow | Melee | Melee | User | -3 | D3 | You can re-roll failed hit rolls for this weapon. |

| ABILITIES | |
|---|---|
| **Living Metal** (pg 82) <br><br> **Master Chronomancer:** Friendly **SAUTEKH INFANTRY** units within 6" of Orikan the Diviner have a 5+ invulnerable save. <br><br> **Technomancer:** Add 1 to Reanimation Protocols rolls for models from **SAUTEKH** units within 3" of any friendly **SAUTEKH CRYPTEKS**. | **The Stars Are Right:** Roll a D6 at the start of each of your turns. If the result is less than the current battle round number, Orikan uses the Orikan Empowered profile for the rest of the game (though any damage he has sustained is carried over). |

| FACTION KEYWORDS | **NECRONS, SAUTEKH** |
|---|---|
| KEYWORDS | **CHARACTER, INFANTRY, CRYPTEK, ORIKAN THE DIVINER** |

# ANRAKYR THE TRAVELLER

**9 POWER**

| NAME | M | WS | BS | S | T | W | A | Ld | Sv |
|------|---|----|----|----|---|---|---|----|----|
| Anrakyr the Traveller | 5" | 2+ | 2+ | 6 | 5 | 6 | 3 | 10 | 3+ |

Anrakyr the Traveller is a single model armed with a tachyon arrow and warscythe. Only one of this model may be included in your army.

| WEAPON | RANGE | TYPE | S | AP | D | ABILITIES |
|--------|-------|------|---|----|----|-----------|
| Tachyon arrow | 120" | Assault 1 | 10 | -5 | D6 | This weapon can only be used once per battle. |
| Warscythe | Melee | Melee | +2 | -4 | 2 | - |

| ABILITIES | |
|-----------|--|
| **Living Metal** (pg 82)<br><br>**Lord of the Pyrrhian Legions:** Add 1 to the Attacks characteristic of friendly **NECRONS INFANTRY** units within 3" of Anrakyr the Traveller.<br><br>**Mind in the Machine:** At the start of your Shooting phase, choose an enemy **VEHICLE** model within 12" of Anrakyr the Traveller and roll a D6. On a 4+, choose one of that vehicle's weapons. You may shoot with that weapon at another enemy unit. The weapon fires using the vehicle's Ballistic Skill. | **Phase Shifter:** Anrakyr the Traveller has a 4+ invulnerable save.<br><br>**My Will Be Done:** At the beginning of your turn, choose a friendly **NECRONS INFANTRY** unit within 6" of Anrakyr the Traveller. Add 1 to Advance, charge and hit rolls for that unit until the beginning of your next turn. A unit can only be chosen as the target of this ability once in each turn. |

| FACTION KEYWORDS | NECRONS |
|------------------|---------|
| **KEYWORDS** | **CHARACTER, INFANTRY, OVERLORD, ANRAKYR THE TRAVELLER** |

# TRAZYN THE INFINITE

**5 POWER**

| NAME | M | WS | BS | S | T | W | A | Ld | Sv |
|------|---|----|----|----|---|---|---|----|----|
| Trazyn the Infinite | 5" | 2+ | 2+ | 5 | 5 | 6 | 3 | 10 | 3+ |

Trazyn the Infinite is a single model armed with the Empathic Obliterator. Only one of this model may be included in your army.

| WEAPON | RANGE | TYPE | S | AP | D | ABILITIES |
|--------|-------|------|---|----|----|-----------|
| Empathic Obliterator | Melee | Melee | +2 | -1 | D3 | If a **CHARACTER** is slain by an attack from this weapon, each enemy unit within 6" of the slain character suffers D3 mortal wounds. |

| ABILITIES | |
|-----------|--|
| **Living Metal** (pg 82)<br><br>**Phase Shifter:** Trazyn the Infinite has a 4+ invulnerable save.<br><br>**My Will Be Done:** At the beginning of your turn, choose a friendly **NIHILAKH INFANTRY** unit within 6" of Trazyn the Infinite. Add 1 to Advance, charge and hit rolls for that unit until the beginning of your next turn. A unit can only be chosen as the target of this ability once in each turn. | **Surrogate Hosts:** If Trazyn the Infinite is slain, roll a D6. On a 2+, you may choose another friendly **NECRONS INFANTRY CHARACTER** (other than **CHARACTERS** that you can only include once in your army). Remove that model as if it were slain and place Trazyn in its place with D3 wounds remaining. If no such **CHARACTERS** remain, or you rolled a 1, remove Trazyn the Infinite as a casualty as normal. |

| FACTION KEYWORDS | NECRONS, NIHILAKH |
|------------------|-------------------|
| **KEYWORDS** | **CHARACTER, INFANTRY, OVERLORD, TRAZYN THE INFINITE** |

# CATACOMB COMMAND BARGE

| NAME | M | WS | BS | S | T | W | A | Ld | Sv |
|------|---|----|----|---|---|---|---|----|----|
| Catacomb Command Barge | 12" | 2+ | 2+ | 5 | 6 | 8 | 3 | 10 | 3+ |

A Catacomb Command Barge is a single model equipped with a gauss cannon. It is ridden by an Overlord armed with a staff of light.

| WEAPON | RANGE | TYPE | S | AP | D | ABILITIES |
|--------|-------|------|---|----|----|-----------|
| Gauss cannon | 24" | Heavy 3 | 6 | -3 | D3 | - |
| Staff of light (shooting) | 12" | Assault 3 | 5 | -2 | 1 | - |
| Tesla cannon | 24" | Assault 3 | 6 | 0 | 1 | Each hit roll of 6+ with this weapon causes 3 hits instead of 1. |
| Hyperphase sword | Melee | Melee | +1 | -3 | 1 | - |
| Staff of light (melee) | Melee | Melee | User | -2 | 1 | - |
| Voidblade | Melee | Melee | User | -3 | 1 | Each time the bearer fights, it can make 1 additional attack with this weapon. |
| Warscythe | Melee | Melee | +2 | -4 | 2 | - |

| WARGEAR OPTIONS |
|-----------------|
| • The Overlord may replace their staff of light with a hyperphase sword, a voidblade or a warscythe. |
| • The Overlord may take a resurrection orb. |
| • The Catacomb Command Barge may replace its gauss cannon with a tesla cannon. |

| ABILITIES | |
|-----------|---|
| **Living Metal** (pg 82)<br><br>**Wave of Command:** At the beginning of your turn, choose a friendly <DYNASTY> INFANTRY unit within 12" of this model. Add 1 to Advance, charge and hit rolls for that unit until the beginning of your next turn. A unit can only be chosen as the target of Wave of Command or My Will Be Done once in each turn.<br><br>**Quantum Shielding:** Each time this model fails a saving throw, roll a D6. If the result is less than the damage inflicted by that attack, the damage is ignored (e.g. if this model suffers 4 damage, if you then roll a 3 or less the damage is ignored). Quantum Shielding cannot prevent damage caused by mortal wounds. | **Resurrection Orb:** If this model has a resurrection orb, once per battle, immediately after you have made your Reanimation Protocols rolls at the beginning of the turn, you can make Reanimation Protocols rolls for models from a friendly <DYNASTY> INFANTRY unit within 3" of this model.<br><br>**Explodes:** If this model is reduced to 0 wounds, roll a D6 before removing it from the battlefield. On a 6 it explodes, and each unit within 3" suffers a mortal wound. |

| FACTION KEYWORDS | NECRONS, <DYNASTY> |
|------------------|--------------------|
| KEYWORDS | CHARACTER, VEHICLE, OVERLORD, FLY, CATACOMB COMMAND BARGE |

# OVERLORD

**6 POWER**

| NAME | M | WS | BS | S | T | W | A | Ld | Sv |
|------|---|----|----|---|---|---|---|----|----|
| Overlord | 5" | 2+ | 2+ | 5 | 5 | 5 | 3 | 10 | 3+ |

An Overlord is a single model armed with a staff of light.

| WEAPON | RANGE | TYPE | S | AP | D | ABILITIES |
|--------|-------|------|---|----|----|-----------|
| Staff of light (shooting) | 12" | Assault 3 | 5 | -2 | 1 | - |
| Hyperphase sword | Melee | Melee | +1 | -3 | 1 | - |
| Staff of light (melee) | Melee | Melee | User | -2 | 1 | - |
| Voidblade | Melee | Melee | User | -3 | 1 | Each time the bearer fights, it can make 1 additional attack with this weapon. |
| Voidscythe | Melee | Melee | x2 | -4 | 3 | When attacking with this weapon, subtract 1 from the hit roll. |
| Warscythe | Melee | Melee | +2 | -4 | 2 | |

| WARGEAR OPTIONS | • This model may replace its staff of light with a voidscythe, a hyperphase sword, a voidblade or a warscythe.<br>• This model may take a resurrection orb. |
|-----------------|---|

| ABILITIES | Living Metal (pg 82)<br><br>**Resurrection Orb:** If this model has a resurrection orb, once per battle, immediately after you have made your Reanimation Protocols rolls at the beginning of the turn, you can make Reanimation Protocols rolls for models from a friendly <Dynasty> Infantry unit within 3" of this model. | **Phase Shifter:** This model has a 4+ invulnerable save.<br><br>**My Will Be Done:** At the beginning of your turn, choose a friendly <Dynasty> Infantry unit within 6" of this model. Add 1 to Advance, charge and hit rolls for that unit until the beginning of your next turn. A unit can only be chosen as the target of this ability once in each turn. |
|-----------|---|---|

| FACTION KEYWORDS | NECRONS, <DYNASTY> |
|------------------|---|
| KEYWORDS | CHARACTER, INFANTRY, OVERLORD |

---

# LORD

**5 POWER**

| NAME | M | WS | BS | S | T | W | A | Ld | Sv |
|------|---|----|----|---|---|---|---|----|----|
| Lord | 5" | 3+ | 3+ | 5 | 5 | 4 | 3 | 10 | 3+ |

A Lord is a single model armed with a staff of light.

| WEAPON | RANGE | TYPE | S | AP | D | ABILITIES |
|--------|-------|------|---|----|----|-----------|
| Staff of light (shooting) | 12" | Assault 3 | 5 | -2 | 1 | - |
| Hyperphase sword | Melee | Melee | +1 | -3 | 1 | - |
| Staff of light (melee) | Melee | Melee | User | -2 | 1 | - |
| Voidblade | Melee | Melee | User | -3 | 1 | Each time the bearer fights, it can make 1 additional attack with this weapon. |
| Warscythe | Melee | Melee | +2 | -4 | 2 | - |

| WARGEAR OPTIONS | • This model may replace its staff of light with a hyperphase sword, a voidblade or a warscythe.<br>• This model may take a resurrection orb. |
|-----------------|---|

| ABILITIES | Living Metal (pg 82)<br><br>**The Lord's Will:** Re-roll wound rolls of 1 for friendly <Dynasty> Infantry units that are within 6" of this model. | **Resurrection Orb:** If this model has a resurrection orb, once per battle, immediately after you have made your Reanimation Protocols rolls at the beginning of the turn, you can make Reanimation Protocols rolls for models from a friendly <Dynasty> Infantry unit within 3" of this model. |
|-----------|---|---|

| FACTION KEYWORDS | NECRONS, <DYNASTY> |
|------------------|---|
| KEYWORDS | CHARACTER, INFANTRY, LORD |

# CRYPTEK

| NAME | M | WS | BS | S | T | W | A | Ld | Sv |
|---|---|---|---|---|---|---|---|---|---|
| Cryptek | 5" | 3+ | 3+ | 4 | 4 | 4 | 1 | 10 | 4+ |

A Cryptek is a single model armed with a staff of light.

| WEAPON | RANGE | TYPE | S | AP | D | ABILITIES |
|---|---|---|---|---|---|---|
| Staff of light (shooting) | 12" | Assault 3 | 5 | -2 | 1 | - |
| Staff of light (melee) | Melee | Melee | User | -2 | 1 | - |

| WARGEAR OPTIONS | • This model may take either a chronometron or a Canoptek cloak. |
|---|---|

**ABILITIES**

**Living Metal** (pg 82)

**Chronometron:** <Dynasty> Infantry units within 3" of a friendly model with a chronometron have a 5+ invulnerable save against ranged weapons.

**Technomancer:** Add 1 to all Reanimation Protocols rolls for models from <Dynasty> units within 3" of any friendly <Dynasty> Crypteks.

**Canoptek Cloak:** A model equipped with a Canoptek cloak has a Move characteristic of 10" and gains the Fly keyword. In addition, at the start of your turn you can select one friendly <Dynasty> model that has the Living Metal ability and that is within 3" of this model. That model regains D3 lost wounds, rather than 1, from its Living Metal ability.

| FACTION KEYWORDS | Necrons, <Dynasty> |
|---|---|
| KEYWORDS | Character, Infantry, Cryptek |

# DESTROYER LORD

| NAME | M | WS | BS | S | T | W | A | Ld | Sv |
|---|---|---|---|---|---|---|---|---|---|
| Destroyer Lord | 10" | 3+ | 3+ | 5 | 6 | 6 | 4 | 10 | 3+ |

A Destroyer Lord is a single model armed with a staff of light.

| WEAPON | RANGE | TYPE | S | AP | D | ABILITIES |
|---|---|---|---|---|---|---|
| Staff of light (shooting) | 12" | Assault 3 | 5 | -2 | 1 | - |
| Hyperphase sword | Melee | Melee | +1 | -3 | 1 | - |
| Staff of light (melee) | Melee | Melee | User | -2 | 1 | - |
| Voidblade | Melee | Melee | User | -3 | 1 | Each time the bearer fights, it can make 1 additional attack with this weapon. |
| Warscythe | Melee | Melee | +2 | -4 | 2 | - |

| WARGEAR OPTIONS | • This model may replace its staff of light with a hyperphase sword, a voidblade or a warscythe.<br>• This model may take either a phylactery or a resurrection orb. |
|---|---|

**ABILITIES**

**Living Metal** (pg 82)

**Hardwired Hatred:** You can re-roll hit rolls of 1 for this model.

**United in Hatred:** You can re-roll wound rolls of 1 in the Shooting phase for this model and models from friendly <Dynasty> Destroyer and <Dynasty> Heavy Destroyer units within 6".

**Phase Shifter:** This model has a 4+ invulnerable save.

**Phylactery:** A model with a phylactery regains D3 lost wounds at the beginning of your turn, rather than 1, from their Living Metal ability.

**Resurrection Orb:** If this model has a resurrection orb, once per battle, immediately after you have made your Reanimation Protocols rolls at the beginning of the turn, you can make Reanimation Protocols rolls for models from a friendly <Dynasty> Infantry unit within 3" of this model.

| FACTION KEYWORDS | Necrons, <Dynasty> |
|---|---|
| KEYWORDS | Character, Infantry, Fly, Destroyer Lord |

# NECRON WARRIORS

| NAME | M | WS | BS | S | T | W | A | Ld | Sv |
|------|---|----|----|---|---|---|---|----|----|
| Necron Warrior | 5" | 3+ | 3+ | 4 | 4 | 1 | 1 | 10 | 4+ |

This unit contains 10 Necron Warriors. It may include up to 10 additional Necron Warriors (**Power Rating +6**). Each model is armed with a gauss flayer.

| WEAPON | RANGE | TYPE | S | AP | D | ABILITIES |
|--------|-------|------|---|----|----|-----------|
| Gauss flayer | 24" | Rapid Fire 1 | 4 | -1 | 1 | - |
| **ABILITIES** | **Reanimation Protocols** (pg 82) | | | | | |
| **FACTION KEYWORDS** | **NECRONS, <DYNASTY>** | | | | | |
| **KEYWORDS** | **INFANTRY, WARRIORS** | | | | | |

# IMMORTALS

| NAME | M | WS | BS | S | T | W | A | Ld | Sv |
|------|---|----|----|---|---|---|---|----|----|
| Immortal | 5" | 3+ | 3+ | 4 | 4 | 1 | 1 | 10 | 3+ |

This unit contains 5 Immortals. It can include up to 5 additional Immortals (**Power Rating +4**). Each model is armed with a gauss blaster.

| WEAPON | RANGE | TYPE | S | AP | D | ABILITIES |
|--------|-------|------|---|----|----|-----------|
| Gauss blaster | 24" | Rapid Fire 1 | 5 | -2 | 1 | - |
| Tesla carbine | 24" | Assault 2 | 5 | 0 | 1 | Each hit roll of 6+ with this weapon causes 3 hits instead of 1. |
| **WARGEAR OPTIONS** | • The entire unit may replace their gauss blasters with tesla carbines. | | | | | |
| **ABILITIES** | **Reanimation Protocols** (pg 82) | | | | | |
| **FACTION KEYWORDS** | **NECRONS, <DYNASTY>** | | | | | |
| **KEYWORDS** | **INFANTRY, IMMORTALS** | | | | | |

Immortals are battle-hardened veterans who have ground countless stellar empires to dust beneath their relentless march.

# LYCHGUARD

| NAME | M | WS | BS | S | T | W | A | Ld | Sv |
|------|---|----|----|---|---|---|---|----|----|
| Lychguard | 5" | 3+ | 3+ | 5 | 5 | 2 | 2 | 10 | 3+ |

This unit contains 5 Lychguard. It can include up to 5 additional Lychguard (**Power Rating +8**). Each model is armed with a warscythe.

| WEAPON | RANGE | TYPE | S | AP | D | ABILITIES |
|--------|-------|------|---|----|----|-----------|
| Hyperphase sword | Melee | Melee | +1 | -3 | 1 | - |
| Warscythe | Melee | Melee | +2 | -4 | 2 | - |

| WARGEAR OPTIONS | • The entire unit may replace their warscythes with hyperphase swords and dispersion shields. |
|-----------------|--------------------------------------------------------------------------------------------------|

| ABILITIES | Reanimation Protocols (pg 82) | Guardian Protocols: Roll a D6 each time a friendly |
|-----------|-------------------------------|----------------------------------------------------|
| | | **<DYNASTY> CHARACTER** loses a wound whilst they are |
| | **Dispersion Shield:** A model equipped with a | within 3" of this unit; on a 2+ a model from this unit can |
| | dispersion shield has a 4+ invulnerable save. | intercept that hit – the character does not lose a wound |
| | | but this unit suffers a mortal wound. |

| FACTION KEYWORDS | NECRONS, <DYNASTY> |
|------------------|--------------------|
| KEYWORDS | INFANTRY, LYCHGUARD |

# DEATHMARKS

| NAME | M | WS | BS | S | T | W | A | Ld | Sv |
|------|---|----|----|---|---|---|---|----|----|
| Deathmarks | 5" | 3+ | 3+ | 4 | 4 | 1 | 1 | 10 | 3+ |

This unit contains 5 Deathmarks. It can include up to 5 additional Deathmarks (**Power Rating +4**). Each model is armed with a synaptic disintegrator.

| WEAPON | RANGE | TYPE | S | AP | D | ABILITIES |
|--------|-------|------|---|----|----|-----------|
| Synaptic disintegrator | 24" | Rapid Fire 1 | 4 | 0 | 1 | This weapon may target a **CHARACTER** even if it is not the closest enemy unit. Each time you roll a wound roll of 6+ for this weapon, the target suffers a mortal wound in addition to any other damage. |

| ABILITIES | Reanimation Protocols (pg 82) | Ethereal Interception: When an enemy unit is set up |
|-----------|-------------------------------|-----------------------------------------------------|
| | | (other than during deployment or when disembarking) |
| | **Hunters from Hyperspace:** During deployment, you | you can immediately set up a unit of Deathmarks that |
| | can set up this unit in a hyperspace oubliette instead of | was set up in a hyperspace oubliette on the battlefield, |
| | placing it on the battlefield. At the end of any of your | anywhere more than 9" away from any enemy models |
| | Movement phases the Deathmarks can slip back into | and within 12" of the enemy unit that has just been set |
| | reality – set them up anywhere on the battlefield that is | up. You can then make a shooting attack with this unit |
| | more than 9" away from any enemy models. | as if it were your Shooting phase, but this attack must |
| | | target the enemy unit that was just set up. |

| FACTION KEYWORDS | NECRONS, <DYNASTY> |
|------------------|--------------------|
| KEYWORDS | INFANTRY, DEATHMARKS |

'Nemesor Ios has ordered a bold strategic withdrawal, luring the enemy into pursuit and exposing their flank to a swift counter-assault. It falls to the ten of us to hold the pass against the savage hordes and buy the throne barge of His Supreme Celestial Glory time to reposition. Let us be about the task.'

- Lychguard Sutrep, First Scythe of Nemesor Ios

# FLAYED ONES

| NAME | M | WS | BS | S | T | W | A | Ld | Sv |
|------|---|----|----|---|---|---|---|----|----|
| Flayed One | 5" | 3+ | 6+ | 4 | 4 | 1 | 3 | 10 | 4+ |

This unit contains 5 Flayed Ones. It can include up to 5 additional Flayed Ones (**Power Rating +4**), up to 10 additional Flayed Ones (**Power Rating +8**) or up to 15 additional Flayed Ones (**Power Rating +12**). Each model attacks with their flayer claws.

| WEAPON | RANGE | TYPE | S | AP | D | ABILITIES |
|--------|-------|------|---|----|----|-----------|
| Flayer claws | Melee | Melee | User | 0 | 1 | You can re-roll failed wound rolls for this weapon. |

| ABILITIES | |
|-----------|--|
| **Reanimation Protocols** (pg 82)<br><br>**Flesh Hunger:** If any Flayed Ones slay any models in a unit, that unit subtracts 1 from its Leadership characteristic until the end of the turn. | **Haunting Horrors:** During deployment, you can set up this unit in a charnel pocket-dimension instead of placing it on the battlefield. At the end of any of your Movement phases the Flayed Ones can crawl out into reality – set them up anywhere on the battlefield that is more than 9" away from any enemy models. |

| FACTION KEYWORDS | **NECRONS, <DYNASTY>** |
|------------------|------------------------|
| KEYWORDS | **INFANTRY, FLAYED ONES** |

**Driven to savagery by an ancient madness, Flayed Ones delight in tearing the flesh from their prey with razor-sharp talons.**

# TRIARCH PRAETORIANS

| NAME | M | WS | BS | S | T | W | A | Ld | Sv |
|------|---|----|----|---|---|---|---|----|----|
| Triarch Praetorian | 10" | 3+ | 3+ | 5 | 5 | 2 | 2 | 10 | 3+ |

This unit contains 5 Triarch Praetorians. It can include up to 5 additional Triarch Praetorians (**Power Rating +8**). Each model is armed with a rod of covenant.

| WEAPON | RANGE | TYPE | S | AP | D | ABILITIES |
|--------|-------|------|---|----|---|-----------|
| Particle caster | 12" | Pistol 1 | 6 | 0 | 1 | - |
| Rod of covenant (shooting) | 12" | Assault 1 | 5 | -3 | 1 | - |
| Rod of covenant (melee) | Melee | Melee | User | -3 | 1 | - |
| Voidblade | Melee | Melee | User | -3 | 1 | Each time the bearer fights, it can make 1 additional attack with this weapon. |

| WARGEAR OPTIONS | • The entire unit may replace their rods of covenant with voidblades and particle casters. |
|-----------------|-----------------------------------------------------------------------------------------------|

| ABILITIES | Reanimation Protocols (pg 82)<br><br>**A Purpose Unshakeable:** This unit automatically passes Morale tests. |
|-----------|-----------------------------------------------------------------------------------------------------------------|

| FACTION KEYWORDS | NECRONS |
|------------------|---------|

| KEYWORDS | INFANTRY, FLY, TRIARCH PRAETORIANS |
|----------|-------------------------------------|

# TRIARCH STALKER

**DAMAGE**
Some of this model's characteristics change as it suffers damage, as shown below:

| REMAINING W | M | WS | BS |
|-------------|-----|----|----|
| 6-10+ | 10" | 3+ | 3+ |
| 3-5 | 8" | 4+ | 4+ |
| 1-2 | 6" | 5+ | 5+ |

| NAME | M | WS | BS | S | T | W | A | Ld | Sv |
|------|---|----|----|---|---|---|---|----|----|
| Triarch Stalker | * | * | * | 7 | 6 | 10 | 3 | 10 | 3+ |

A Triarch Stalker is a single model equipped with a heat ray and massive forelimbs.

| WEAPON | RANGE | TYPE | S | AP | D | ABILITIES |
|--------|-------|------|---|----|---|-----------|
| Heat ray | When attacking with this weapon, choose one of the profiles below. | | | | | |
| - Dispersed | 8" | Heavy 2D6 | 5 | -1 | 1 | When you use this profile, this weapon automatically hits its target. |
| - Focused | 24" | Heavy 2 | 8 | -4 | D6 | When you use this profile, if the target is within half range, roll two dice when inflicting damage with it and discard the lowest result. |
| Particle shredder | 24" | Heavy 6 | 7 | -1 | D3 | - |
| Twin heavy gauss cannon | 36" | Heavy 2 | 9 | -4 | D6 | - |
| Massive forelimbs | Melee | Melee | User | -1 | D3 | - |

| WARGEAR OPTIONS | • This model may replace its heat ray with a particle shredder or a twin heavy gauss cannon. |
|-----------------|-----------------------------------------------------------------------------------------------|

| ABILITIES | Living Metal (pg 82)<br><br>**Quantum Shielding:** Each time this model fails a saving throw, roll a D6. If the result is less than the damage inflicted by that attack, the damage is ignored (e.g. if this model suffers 4 damage, if you then roll a 3 or less the damage is ignored). Quantum Shielding cannot prevent damage caused by mortal wounds. | **Targeting Relay:** You can re-roll hit rolls of 1 for any friendly NECRONS that make a shooting attack against a unit that has already been attacked by any Triarch Stalkers in this phase.<br><br>**Explodes:** If this model is reduced to 0 wounds, roll a D6 before removing it from the battlefield. On a 6 it explodes, and each unit within 6" suffers D3 mortal wounds. |
|-----------|----|----|

| FACTION KEYWORDS | NECRONS |
|------------------|---------|

| KEYWORDS | VEHICLE, TRIARCH STALKER |
|----------|---------------------------|

**12** POWER

# C'TAN SHARD OF THE DECEIVER

| NAME | M | WS | BS | S | T | W | A | Ld | Sv |
|---|---|---|---|---|---|---|---|---|---|
| C'tan Shard of the Deceiver | 8" | 2+ | 2+ | 7 | 7 | 8 | 4 | 10 | 4+ |

The C'tan Shard of the Deceiver is a single model that attacks with its star-god fists. Only one of this model may be included in your army.

| WEAPON | RANGE | TYPE | S | AP | D | ABILITIES |
|---|---|---|---|---|---|---|
| Star-god fists | Melee | Melee | User | -4 | 3 | - |

| ABILITIES | |
|---|---|
| **Necrodermis:** The C'tan Shard of the Deceiver has a 4+ invulnerable save.<br><br>**Dread:** Your opponent must add 1 to Morale tests for any enemy units within 12" of the C'tan Shard of the Deceiver.<br><br>**Grand Illusion:** At the beginning of the first battle round, but before the first turn begins, you can remove the C'tan Shard of the Deceiver and/or up to D3 other friendly NECRONS units from the battlefield, then set them up again more than 12" from any enemy models. If you do so, these units cannot charge in your first turn. | **Powers of the C'tan:** The C'tan Shard of the Deceiver knows two Powers of the C'tan (pg 113). It can use one of its powers at the end of each of its Movement phases.<br><br>**Reality Unravels:** If the C'tan Shard of the Deceiver is ever reduced to 0 wounds, roll a D6 before removing it from the battlefield; on a 4+ its necrodermis tears a hole in reality, and each unit within 3" suffers D3 mortal wounds.<br><br>**Enslaved Star God:** This model can never have a Warlord Trait. |

| FACTION KEYWORDS | NECRONS, C'TAN SHARDS |
|---|---|
| KEYWORDS | CHARACTER, MONSTER, FLY, C'TAN SHARD OF THE DECEIVER |

**12** POWER

# C'TAN SHARD OF THE NIGHTBRINGER

| NAME | M | WS | BS | S | T | W | A | Ld | Sv |
|---|---|---|---|---|---|---|---|---|---|
| C'tan Shard of the Nightbringer | 8" | 2+ | 2+ | 7 | 7 | 8 | 4 | 10 | 4+ |

The C'tan Shard of the Nightbringer is a single model that attacks with a gaze of death and the Scythe of the Nightbringer. Only one of this model may be included in your army.

| WEAPON | RANGE | TYPE | S | AP | D | ABILITIES |
|---|---|---|---|---|---|---|
| Gaze of death | 12" | Assault D6 | * | -4 | D3 | This weapon wounds on a 2+, unless it is targeting a VEHICLE unit, in which case it wounds on a 6+. |
| Scythe of the Nightbringer | Melee | Melee | * | -4 | D6 | This weapon wounds on a 2+, unless it is targeting a VEHICLE unit, in which case it has a Strength characteristic of 7. |

| ABILITIES | |
|---|---|
| **Necrodermis:** The C'tan Shard of the Nightbringer has a 4+ invulnerable save.<br><br>**Powers of the C'tan:** The C'tan Shard of the Nightbringer knows two Powers of the C'tan (pg 113). It can use one of its powers at the end of each of its Movement phases. | **Reality Unravels:** If the C'tan Shard of the Nightbringer is ever reduced to 0 wounds, roll a D6 before removing it from the battlefield; on a 4+ its necrodermis tears a hole in reality, and each unit within 3" suffers D3 mortal wounds.<br><br>**Enslaved Star God:** This model can never have a Warlord Trait. |

| FACTION KEYWORDS | NECRONS, C'TAN SHARDS |
|---|---|
| KEYWORDS | CHARACTER, MONSTER, FLY, C'TAN SHARD OF THE NIGHTBRINGER |

# CANOPTEK WRAITHS

| NAME | M | WS | BS | S | T | W | A | Ld | Sv |
|---|---|---|---|---|---|---|---|---|---|
| Canoptek Wraith | 12" | 3+ | 3+ | 6 | 5 | 3 | 3 | 10 | 4+ |

This unit contains 3 Canoptek Wraiths. It may include up to 3 additional Canoptek Wraiths (**Power Rating +9**). Each model is equipped with vicious claws.

| WEAPON | RANGE | TYPE | S | AP | D | ABILITIES |
|---|---|---|---|---|---|---|
| Particle caster | 12" | Pistol 1 | 6 | 0 | 1 | - |
| Transdimensional beamer | 12" | Heavy D3 | 4 | -3 | 1 | Each time you roll a wound roll of 6+ for this weapon, the target suffers a mortal wound in addition to any other damage. |
| Vicious claws | Melee | Melee | User | -2 | 2 | - |
| Whip coils | Melee | Melee | User | -2 | 2 | If the bearer is slain in the Fight phase before it has made its attacks, leave the model where it is. When its unit is chosen to fight in that phase, it can do so as normal. Once it has done so, remove the model from the battlefield. |
| WARGEAR OPTIONS | • Any model may take a particle caster, transdimensional beamer or whip coils. |
| ABILITIES | **Wraith Form:** Models in this unit have a 3+ invulnerable save, and can move across models and terrain as if they were not there. Models in this unit can shoot and charge even if they Fell Back this turn. |
| FACTION KEYWORDS | **NECRONS, CANOPTEK, <DYNASTY>** |
| KEYWORDS | **BEASTS, CANOPTEK WRAITHS** |

# CANOPTEK SCARABS

| NAME | M | WS | BS | S | T | W | A | Ld | Sv |
|---|---|---|---|---|---|---|---|---|---|
| Canoptek Scarab Swarm | 10" | 4+ | - | 3 | 3 | 3 | 4 | 10 | 6+ |

This unit contains 3 Canoptek Scarab Swarms. It may include up to 3 additional Canoptek Scarab Swarms (**Power Rating +2**) or up to 6 additional Canoptek Scarab Swarms (**Power Rating +4**). Each swarm is equipped with feeder mandibles.

| WEAPON | RANGE | TYPE | S | AP | D | ABILITIES |
|---|---|---|---|---|---|---|
| Feeder mandibles | Melee | Melee | User | 0 | 1 | If the target's Toughness is higher than this attack's Strength, this weapon always wounds the target on a wound roll of 5+. |
| FACTION KEYWORDS | **NECRONS, CANOPTEK, <DYNASTY>** |
| KEYWORDS | **SWARM, FLY, CANOPTEK SCARABS** |

Canoptek Scarabs sweep over the enemy in a clicking, scuttling tide, tearing open flesh and armour with their razor-sharp jaws.

# TOMB BLADES

**5 POWER**

| NAME | M | WS | BS | S | T | W | A | Ld | Sv |
|---|---|---|---|---|---|---|---|---|---|
| Tomb Blades | 14" | 3+ | 3+ | 4 | 5 | 2 | 1 | 10 | 4+ |

This unit contains 3 Tomb Blades. It can include up to 3 additional Tomb Blades (**Power Rating +5**) or up to 6 additional Tomb Blades (**Power Rating +9**). Each model is equipped with two gauss blasters.

| WEAPON | RANGE | TYPE | S | AP | D | ABILITIES |
|---|---|---|---|---|---|---|
| Gauss blaster | 24" | Rapid Fire 1 | 5 | -2 | 1 | - |
| Particle beamer | 24" | Assault 3 | 6 | 0 | 1 | - |
| Tesla carbine | 24" | Assault 2 | 5 | 0 | 1 | Each hit roll of 6+ with this weapon causes 3 hits instead of 1. |

| WARGEAR OPTIONS | • Any model may replace its two gauss blasters with two tesla carbines or a particle beamer.<br>• Any model may take shieldvanes.<br>• Any model may take a nebuloscope or a shadowloom. |
|---|---|

| ABILITIES | **Reanimation Protocols** (pg 82)<br><br>**Evasion Engrams:** Your opponent must subtract 1 from hit rolls that target this unit in the Shooting phase.<br><br>**Shieldvanes:** A model with shieldvanes has a Save characteristic of 3+. | **Shadowloom:** A model with a shadowloom has a 5+ invulnerable save.<br><br>**Nebuloscope:** Models do not receive the bonus to their save for being in cover against attacks made by a model with a nebuloscope. |
|---|---|---|

| FACTION KEYWORDS | NECRONS, <DYNASTY> |
|---|---|
| KEYWORDS | BIKER, FLY, TOMB BLADES |

# DESTROYERS

**3 POWER**

| NAME | M | WS | BS | S | T | W | A | Ld | Sv |
|---|---|---|---|---|---|---|---|---|---|
| Destroyer | 10" | 3+ | 3+ | 4 | 5 | 3 | 2 | 10 | 3+ |
| Heavy Destroyer | 10" | 3+ | 3+ | 4 | 5 | 3 | 2 | 10 | 3+ |

This unit contains 1 Destroyer. It can include up to 5 additional Destroyers (**Power Rating +3 per model**). If the unit contains at least three models, a Heavy Destroyer can take the place of a Destroyer.
• Each Destroyer is armed with a gauss cannon.
• The Heavy Destroyer is armed with a heavy gauss cannon.

| WEAPON | RANGE | TYPE | S | AP | D | ABILITIES |
|---|---|---|---|---|---|---|
| Gauss cannon | 24" | Heavy 3 | 6 | -3 | D3 | - |
| Heavy gauss cannon | 36" | Heavy 1 | 9 | -4 | D6 | - |

| ABILITIES | **Reanimation Protocols** (pg 82)<br><br>**Hardwired Hatred:** You can re-roll hit rolls of 1 for this unit. | **Repulsor Platform:** This unit can move and fire Heavy weapons without suffering the penalty to its hit rolls. |
|---|---|---|

| FACTION KEYWORDS | NECRONS, <DYNASTY> |
|---|---|
| KEYWORDS | INFANTRY, FLY, DESTROYERS |

'The Destroyers? They are weapons, nothing more, and should be expended as such. They are Necron in form only, having been reborn to a madness deeper than anything to which I have borne witness. Whilst I hold nothing but admiration for their drive and efficiency, I can present no logic adequate to justify their ultimate goal. A warrior's proper function is to fight for a profound objective, to leave behind works or deeds greater than himself. Given free reign, the Destroyers would leave behind nothing: not life, nor art, nor glory. Only dust would remain. I am a soulless machine, yet even I feel pity for their victims.'

*- Szarekh, Last of the Silent Kings*

# HEAVY DESTROYERS

**3** POWER

| NAME | M | WS | BS | S | T | W | A | Ld | Sv |
|------|---|----|----|----|----|----|----|----|----|
| Heavy Destroyer | 10" | 3+ | 3+ | 4 | 5 | 3 | 2 | 10 | 3+ |

This unit contains 1 Heavy Destroyer. It may include 1 additional Heavy Destroyer (**Power Rating +3**) or 2 additional Heavy Destroyers (**Power Rating +6**). Each model is armed with a heavy gauss cannon.

| WEAPON | RANGE | TYPE | S | AP | D | ABILITIES |
|--------|-------|------|---|----|----|-----------|
| Heavy gauss cannon | 36" | Heavy 1 | 9 | -4 | D6 | - |

| ABILITIES | |
|-----------|--|
| **Reanimation Protocols** (pg 82) <br><br> **Hardwired Hatred:** You can re-roll hit rolls of 1 for this unit. | **Repulsor Platform:** This unit can move and fire Heavy weapons without suffering the penalty to its hit rolls. |

| FACTION KEYWORDS | NECRONS, <DYNASTY> |
|------------------|--------------------|
| KEYWORDS | INFANTRY, FLY, HEAVY DESTROYERS |

# CANOPTEK SPYDERS

**4** POWER

| NAME | M | WS | BS | S | T | W | A | Ld | Sv |
|------|---|----|----|----|----|----|----|----|----|
| Canoptek Spyders | 6" | 4+ | 4+ | 6 | 6 | 4 | 4 | 10 | 3+ |

This unit contains 1 Canoptek Spyder. It may include 1 additional Canoptek Spyder (**Power Rating +4**) or 2 additional Canoptek Spyders (**Power Rating +8**). Each model is equipped with automaton claws.

| WEAPON | RANGE | TYPE | S | AP | D | ABILITIES |
|--------|-------|------|---|----|----|-----------|
| Particle beamer | 24" | Assault 3 | 6 | 0 | 1 | - |
| Automaton claws | Melee | Melee | User | -2 | D3 | - |

| WARGEAR OPTIONS | <ul><li>Any model may take a fabricator claw array.</li><li>Any model may take a gloom prism.</li><li>Any model may take two particle beamers.</li></ul> |
|-----------------|--|

| ABILITIES | |
|-----------|--|
| **Fabricator Claw Array:** At the end of your Movement phase a model equipped with a fabricator claw array can repair a single <DYNASTY> VEHICLE model within 1". That model regains D3 wounds lost earlier in the battle. A model can only be repaired once per turn. <br><br> **Gloom Prism:** A model equipped with a gloom prism can attempt to deny one psychic power in each enemy Psychic phase in the same manner as a PSYKER. | **Scarab Hive:** At the beginning of your turn, you can roll a D6 for each <DYNASTY> Canoptek Scarabs unit from your army that is below its starting number of models and within 6" of any friendly <DYNASTY> Canoptek Spyders units. On a 1, one of those Canoptek Spyders units within 6" of the unit being rolled for suffers a mortal wound. On a 2+ one of those Canoptek Spyders units within 6" of the unit being rolled for unleashes reinforcements: return a Canoptek Scarab Swarm to the depleted unit, in unit coherency and more than 1" from enemy models. If you cannot do this because there is no room to place the model, do not set it up. |

| FACTION KEYWORDS | NECRONS, CANOPTEK, <DYNASTY> |
|------------------|------------------------------|
| KEYWORDS | MONSTER, FLY, CANOPTEK SPYDERS |

# MONOLITH

A Monolith is a single model equipped with four gauss flux arcs and a particle whip.

| NAME | M | WS | BS | S | T | W | A | Ld | Sv |
|---|---|---|---|---|---|---|---|---|---|
| Monolith | * | 6+ | * | 8 | 8 | 20 | 3 | 10 | 3+ |

| WEAPON | RANGE | TYPE | S | AP | D | ABILITIES |
|---|---|---|---|---|---|---|
| Gauss flux arc | 24" | Heavy 3 | 5 | -2 | 1 | - |
| Particle whip | 24" | Heavy 6 | 8 | -2 | D3 | - |

## DAMAGE

Some of this model's characteristics change as it suffers damage, as shown below:

| REMAINING W | M | BS | PORTAL OF EXILE |
|---|---|---|---|
| 11-20+ | 6" | 3+ | 4+ |
| 6-10 | 5" | 4+ | 5+ |
| 1-5 | 4" | 5+ | 6 |

## ABILITIES

**Living Metal** (pg 82)

**Death Descending:** During deployment, you can set up this model in the upper atmosphere instead of placing it on the battlefield. At the end of any of your Movement phases the Monolith can plummet to the battlefield – set it up anywhere on the battlefield that is more than 12" from any enemy models.

**Portal of Exile:** When an enemy unit (other than a **Monster** or **Vehicle**) finishes a charge move within 1" of this model, its portal of exile may activate. Roll a D6 and compare it to the value required on the damage table above. If the roll is successful, the charging unit suffers D6 mortal wounds.

**Hovering:** Distance and ranges are always measured to and from this model's hull, even though it has a base.

**Floating Fortress:** This model can move and fire Heavy weapons without suffering the penalty to its hit rolls.

**Eternity Gate:** When you set up this model, at the same time you can also set up any number of friendly <**Dynasty**> **Infantry** units on their tomb world rather than setting them up on the battlefield. Before this model moves in your Movement phase, a single friendly <**Dynasty**> unit that was set up on their tomb world can be transported onto the battlefield by the Monolith. Set up the unit so that it is wholly within 3" of this model and more than 1" from any enemy models. If all <**Dynasty**> Night Scythes and Monoliths from your army are destroyed, any friendly <**Dynasty**> units still on their tomb world are considered to be slain.

**Explodes:** If this model is reduced to 0 wounds, roll a D6 before removing it from the battlefield. On a 6 it explodes, and each unit within 6" suffers D6 mortal wounds.

| FACTION KEYWORDS | **Necrons**, <**Dynasty**> |
|---|---|
| KEYWORDS | **Vehicle, Titanic, Fly, Monolith** |

The Monolith is a terrifying symbol of Necron dominance, a floating fortress that calls forth rank after rank of soulless warriors.

# ANNIHILATION BARGE

**8 POWER**

| NAME | M | WS | BS | S | T | W | A | Ld | Sv |
|---|---|---|---|---|---|---|---|---|---|
| Annihilation Barge | 12" | 6+ | 3+ | 5 | 6 | 8 | 3 | 10 | 4+ |

An Annihilation Barge is a single model equipped with a gauss cannon and a twin tesla destructor.

| WEAPON | RANGE | TYPE | S | AP | D | ABILITIES |
|---|---|---|---|---|---|---|
| Gauss cannon | 24" | Heavy 3 | 6 | -3 | D3 | - |
| Twin tesla destructor | 24" | Assault 8 | 7 | 0 | 1 | Each hit roll of 6+ with this weapon causes 3 hits instead of 1. |
| Tesla cannon | 24" | Assault 3 | 6 | 0 | 1 | Each hit roll of 6+ with this weapon causes 3 hits instead of 1. |

| WARGEAR OPTIONS | • This model may replace its gauss cannon with a tesla cannon. |
|---|---|

| ABILITIES | **Living Metal** (pg 82)<br><br>**Quantum Shielding:** Each time this model fails a saving throw, roll a D6. If the result is less than the damage inflicted by that attack, the damage is ignored (e.g. if this model suffers 4 damage, if you then roll a 3 or less the damage is ignored). Quantum Shielding cannot prevent damage caused by mortal wounds. | **Explodes:** If this model is reduced to 0 wounds, roll a D6 before removing it from the battlefield. On a 6 it explodes, and each unit within 3" suffers a mortal wound. |
|---|---|---|
| FACTION KEYWORDS | **NECRONS, <DYNASTY>** | |
| KEYWORDS | **VEHICLE, FLY, ANNIHILATION BARGE** | |

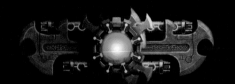

# DOOMSDAY ARK

**10 POWER**

| NAME | M | WS | BS | S | T | W | A | Ld | Sv |
|---|---|---|---|---|---|---|---|---|---|
| Doomsday Ark | * | 6+ | * | 6 | 6 | 14 | * | 10 | 4+ |

**DAMAGE**
Some of this model's characteristics change as it suffers damage, as shown below:

| REMAINING W | M | BS | A |
|---|---|---|---|
| 8-14+ | 12" | 3+ | 3 |
| 4-7 | 8" | 4+ | D3 |
| 1-3 | 4" | 5+ | 1 |

A Doomsday Ark is a single model equipped with a doomsday cannon and two gauss flayer arrays.

| WEAPON | RANGE | TYPE | S | AP | D | ABILITIES |
|---|---|---|---|---|---|---|
| Doomsday cannon | When attacking with this weapon, choose one of the profiles below. | | | | | |
| - Low power | 36" | Heavy D6 | 8 | -2 | D3 | - |
| - High power | 72" | Heavy D6 | 10 | -5 | D6 | A model can only fire the doomsday cannon at high power if it remained stationary in its preceding Movement phase. |
| Gauss flayer array | 24" | Rapid Fire 5 | 4 | -1 | 1 | - |

| ABILITIES | **Living Metal** (pg 82)<br><br>**Explodes:** If this model is reduced to 0 wounds, roll a D6 before removing it from the battlefield. On a 6 it explodes, and each unit within 6" suffers D3 mortal wounds.<br><br>**Hovering:** Instead of measuring distance and ranges to and from this model's base, measure to and from this model's hull or base (whichever is closer). | **Quantum Shielding:** Each time this model fails a saving throw, roll a D6. If the result is less than the damage inflicted by that attack, the damage is ignored (e.g. if this model suffers 4 damage, if you then roll a 3 or less the damage is ignored). Quantum Shielding cannot prevent damage caused by mortal wounds. |
|---|---|---|
| FACTION KEYWORDS | **NECRONS, <DYNASTY>** | |
| KEYWORDS | **VEHICLE, FLY, DOOMSDAY ARK** | |

# TRANSCENDENT C'TAN

| NAME | M | WS | BS | S | T | W | A | Ld | Sv |
|------|---|----|----|---|---|---|---|----|----|
| Transcendent C'tan | 8" | 2+ | 2+ | 7 | 7 | 8 | 4 | 10 | 4+ |

A Transcendent C'tan is a single model that attacks with its crackling tendrils.

| WEAPON | RANGE | TYPE | S | AP | D | ABILITIES |
|--------|-------|------|---|----|----|-----------|
| Crackling tendrils | Melee | Melee | User | -4 | D6 | - |

**ABILITIES**

**Necrodermis:** This model has a 4+ invulnerable save.

**Powers of the C'tan:** This model knows two Powers of the C'tan (pg 113). It can use one of its powers at the end of each of its Movement phases.

**Reality Unravels:** If this model is ever reduced to 0 wounds, roll a D6 before removing it from the battlefield; on a 4+ its necrodermis tears a hole in reality, and each unit within 3" suffers D3 mortal wounds.

**Enslaved Star God:** This model can never have a Warlord Trait.

**Fractured Personality:** Before the battle, you can pick one of the abilities opposite to apply to this model for the duration of the battle. Alternatively, you can roll two D6 to randomly determine two abilities and apply them both to this model for the duration of the battle (duplicate results have no effect).

| D6 | Ability |
|----|---------|
| 1 | **Cosmic Tyrant:** This model can use two different Powers of the C'tan at the end of each of your Movement phases, instead of only one. |
| 2 | **Immune to Natural Law:** Add 1 to saving throws made for this model. |
| 3 | **Sentient Necrodermis:** This model regains D3 lost wounds at the start of each of your turns. |
| 4 | **Transdimensional Displacement:** When this model Advances, add 12" to its Move characteristic for that Movement phase instead of rolling a dice. |
| 5 | **Entropic Touch:** You can re-roll failed wound rolls for this model in the Fight phase. |
| 6 | **Writhing Worldscape:** Enemy units do not receive a bonus to their saving throws for being in cover whilst they are within 12" of this model. |

**FACTION KEYWORDS** | NECRONS, C'TAN SHARDS

**KEYWORDS** | CHARACTER, MONSTER, FLY, TRANSCENDENT C'TAN

'Verminous beasts poured through the breach in their multitudes, dragging my warriors down and peeling open their metal bodies. It was then that I ordered the C'tan set loose, for I would not lose another servant to these base creatures. N'phoran the Spiral Flame emerged upon the battlefield in an explosion of blinding light. It raised a hand dismissively, and in an instant a score of scuttling beasts were unmade, transmuted into a cloud of dust and scattered atoms. Aliens swarmed over the C'tan's blazing form, bodies melting away even as they tried in vain to breach its necrodermis. One of the aliens' weapon-beasts hove into view, its spine glowing with phosphorescent light as it prepared to fire its organic cannon. N'phoran clenched a fist, and a meteor of black fire burst from its outstretched hand and struck the monster's head, crushing its skull in an explosion of bone and ichor.'

*- Nemesor Yhardusz, the Spear of Karsa*

# GHOST ARK

| NAME | M | WS | BS | S | T | W | A | Ld | Sv |
|---|---|---|---|---|---|---|---|---|---|
| Ghost Ark | * | 6+ | * | 6 | 6 | 14 | * | 10 | 4+ |

A Ghost Ark is a single model equipped with two gauss flayer arrays.

**DAMAGE**

Some of this model's characteristics change as it suffers damage, as shown below:

| REMAINING W | M | BS | A |
|---|---|---|---|
| 8-14+ | 12" | 3+ | 3 |
| 4-7 | 8" | 4+ | D3 |
| 1-3 | 4" | 5+ | 1 |

| WEAPON | RANGE | TYPE | S | AP | D | ABILITIES |
|---|---|---|---|---|---|---|
| Gauss flayer array | 24" | Rapid Fire 5 | 4 | -1 | 1 | - |

| ABILITIES | Living Metal (pg 82) | |
|---|---|---|

**Quantum Shielding:** Each time this model fails a saving throw, roll a D6. If the result is less than the damage inflicted by that attack, the damage is ignored (e.g. if this model suffers 4 damage, if you then roll a 3 or less the damage is ignored). Quantum Shielding cannot prevent damage caused by mortal wounds.

**Hovering:** Instead of measuring distance and ranges to and from this model's base, measure to and from this model's hull or base (whichever is closer).

**Explodes:** If this model is reduced to 0 wounds, roll a D6 before removing it from the battlefield and before any units disembark. On a 6 it explodes, and each unit within 6" suffers D3 mortal wounds.

**Repair Barge:** You can make Reanimation Protocols rolls for any slain models from units embarked on a Ghost Ark, even though those units are not on the battlefield. Any models returned to the unit this way are added to the number of models embarked on the Ghost Ark – if any models cannot be returned because there is no more room on the Ghost Ark, they are not returned this turn. In addition, at the end of your Movement phase, you can make Reanimation Protocols rolls for slain models from <DYNASTY> Warriors units within 3" of any friendly <DYNASTY> Ghost Arks. You cannot use this ability on a unit that has been the target of a resurrection orb or the Orb of Eternity this turn.

| TRANSPORT | This model can transport 10 <DYNASTY> INFANTRY models, which must be Warriors or CHARACTERS. It cannot transport Destroyer Lords. |
|---|---|
| FACTION KEYWORDS | NECRONS, <DYNASTY> |
| KEYWORDS | VEHICLE, TRANSPORT, FLY, GHOST ARK |

Ghost Arks soar ominously over the battlefield, deploying rank after rank of silent, soulless warriors into the fray.

# DOOM SCYTHE

**11 POWER**

| NAME | M | WS | BS | S | T | W | A | Ld | Sv |
|------|---|----|----|---|---|---|---|----|----|
| Doom Scythe | * | 6+ | * | 6 | 6 | 12 | * | 10 | 3+ |

A Doom Scythe is a single model equipped with a death ray and two tesla destructors.

**DAMAGE**
Some of this model's characteristics change as it suffers damage, as shown below:

| REMAINING W | M | BS | A |
|-------------|---|----|---|
| 7-12+ | 20-60" | 3+ | 3 |
| 4-6 | 20-40" | 4+ | D3 |
| 1-3 | 20-25" | 5+ | 1 |

| WEAPON | RANGE | TYPE | S | AP | D | ABILITIES |
|--------|-------|------|---|----|----|-----------|
| Death ray | 24" | Heavy D3 | 10 | -4 | D6 | - |
| Tesla destructor | 24" | Assault 4 | 7 | 0 | 1 | Each hit roll of 6+ with this weapon causes 3 hits instead of 1. |

| ABILITIES | |
|-----------|--|
| **Living Metal** (pg 82)<br><br>**Airborne:** This model cannot charge, can only be charged by units that can **FLY**, and can only attack or be attacked in the Fight phase by units that can **FLY**.<br><br>**Hard to Hit:** Your opponent must subtract 1 from hit rolls for attacks that target this model in the Shooting phase. | **Supersonic:** Each time this model moves, first pivot it on the spot up to 90° (this does not contribute to how far the model moves), and then move the model straight forwards. Note that it cannot pivot again after the initial pivot. When this model Advances, increase its Move characteristic by 20" until the end of the phase – do not roll a dice.<br><br>**Crash and Burn:** If this model is reduced to 0 wounds, roll a D6 before removing it from the battlefield. On a 6 it crashes in a fiery explosion and each unit within 6" suffers D3 mortal wounds. |

| FACTION KEYWORDS | NECRONS, <DYNASTY> |
|------------------|---------------------|
| KEYWORDS | VEHICLE, FLY, DOOM SCYTHE |

---

# NIGHT SCYTHE

**8 POWER**

| NAME | M | WS | BS | S | T | W | A | Ld | Sv |
|------|---|----|----|---|---|---|---|----|----|
| Night Scythe | * | 6+ | * | 6 | 6 | 12 | * | 10 | 3+ |

A Night Scythe is a single model equipped with two tesla destructors.

**DAMAGE**
Some of this model's characteristics change as it suffers damage, as shown below:

| REMAINING W | M | BS | A |
|-------------|---|----|---|
| 7-12+ | 20-60" | 3+ | 3 |
| 4-6 | 20-40" | 4+ | D3 |
| 1-3 | 20-25" | 5+ | 1 |

| WEAPON | RANGE | TYPE | S | AP | D | ABILITIES |
|--------|-------|------|---|----|----|-----------|
| Tesla destructor | 24" | Assault 4 | 7 | 0 | 1 | Each hit roll of 6+ with this weapon causes 3 hits instead of 1. |

| ABILITIES | |
|-----------|--|
| **Living Metal** (pg 82)<br><br>**Airborne:** This model cannot charge, can only be charged by units that can **FLY**, and can only attack or be attacked in the Fight phase by units that can **FLY**.<br><br>**Hard to Hit:** Your opponent must subtract 1 from hit rolls for attacks that target this model in the Shooting phase.<br><br>**Supersonic:** Each time this model moves, first pivot it on the spot up to 90° (this does not contribute to how far the model moves), and then move the model straight forwards. Note that it cannot pivot again after the initial pivot. When this model Advances, increase its Move characteristic by 20" until the end of the phase – do not roll a dice. | **Crash and Burn:** If this model is reduced to 0 wounds, roll a D6 before removing it from the battlefield. On a 6 it crashes in a fiery explosion and each unit within 6" suffers D3 mortal wounds.<br><br>**Invasion Beams:** When you set up this model, at the same time you can also set up any number of friendly <DYNASTY> INFANTRY units on their tomb world rather than setting them up on the battlefield. Before this model moves in your Movement phase, a single friendly <DYNASTY> unit that was set up on their tomb world can be beamed onto the battlefield by the Night Scythe. Set up the unit so that it is wholly within 3" of this model and more than 1" from any enemy models. If all <DYNASTY> Night Scythes and Monoliths from your army are destroyed, any friendly <DYNASTY> units still on their tomb world are considered to be slain. |

| FACTION KEYWORDS | NECRONS, <DYNASTY> |
|------------------|---------------------|
| KEYWORDS | VEHICLE, FLY, NIGHT SCYTHE |

## OBELISK

**22 POWER**

| NAME | M | WS | BS | S | T | W | A | Ld | Sv |
|------|---|----|----|---|---|---|---|----|----|
| Obelisk | * | 6+ | * | 8 | 8 | 24 | 3 | 10 | 3+ |

An Obelisk is a single model equipped with four tesla spheres.

| WEAPON | RANGE | TYPE | S | AP | D | ABILITIES |
|--------|-------|------|---|----|----|-----------|
| Tesla sphere | 24" | Assault 5 | 7 | 0 | 1 | Each hit roll of 6+ with this weapon causes 3 hits instead of 1. |

**DAMAGE**

Some of this model's characteristics change as it suffers damage, as shown below:

| REMAINING W | M | BS | GRAVITY PULSE |
|-------------|---|----|----|
| 13-24+ | 8" | 3+ | 18" |
| 7-12 | 6" | 4+ | 12" |
| 1-6 | 4" | 5+ | 6" |

**ABILITIES**

**Living Metal** (pg 82)

**Hovering Sentinel:** During deployment, you can set up this model in the upper atmosphere instead of placing it on the battlefield. At the end of any of your Movement phases the Obelisk can plummet to the battlefield – set it up anywhere on the battlefield that is more than 12" from any enemy models.

**Gravity Pulse:** At the start of your Shooting phase, roll a D6 for each enemy unit that can **FLY** and is within the distance specified on the damage table above. On a roll of 6, that unit suffers D3 mortal wounds.

**Explodes:** If this model is reduced to 0 wounds, roll a D6 before removing it from the battlefield. On a 6 it explodes, and each unit within 2D6" suffers D6 mortal wounds.

| FACTION KEYWORDS | NECRONS, <DYNASTY> |
|------------------|--------------------|
| KEYWORDS | VEHICLE, TITANIC, FLY, OBELISK |

---

## TESSERACT VAULT

**25 POWER**

| NAME | M | WS | BS | S | T | W | A | Ld | Sv |
|------|---|----|----|---|---|---|---|----|----|
| Tesseract Vault | * | 6+ | * | 8 | 7 | 28 | 3 | 10 | 3+ |

A Tesseract Vault is a single model equipped with four tesla spheres.

| WEAPON | RANGE | TYPE | S | AP | D | ABILITIES |
|--------|-------|------|---|----|----|-----------|
| Tesla sphere | 24" | Assault 5 | 7 | 0 | 1 | Each hit roll of 6+ with this weapon causes 3 hits instead of 1. |

**DAMAGE**

Some of this model's characteristics change as it suffers damage, as shown below:

| REMAINING W | M | BS | POWERS OF THE C'TAN |
|-------------|---|----|----|
| 15-28+ | 8" | 3+ | 3 |
| 8-14 | 6" | 4+ | 2 |
| 1-7 | 4" | 5+ | 1 |

**ABILITIES**

**Living Metal** (pg 82)

**Powers of the C'tan:** This model knows four Powers of the C'tan (pg 113). It can use a number of different Powers of the C'tan equal to the number in the damage table above at the end of each of your Movement phases.

**Transtemporal Force Field:** This model has a 4+ invulnerable save.

**Vengeance of the Enchained:** If this model is reduced to 0 wounds, roll a D6 before removing it from the battlefield. On a 4+ the Transcendent C'tan contained within takes their vengeance, and each unit within 2D6" suffers D6 mortal wounds.

| FACTION KEYWORDS | NECRONS, C'TAN SHARDS, <DYNASTY> |
|------------------|--------------------|
| KEYWORDS | VEHICLE, TITANIC, FLY, TESSERACT VAULT |

# ARMOURY OF THE ANCIENTS

Necron weapons are techno-arcane marvels that harness technologies beyond the ken of most of the younger races. When unleashed they wreak unspeakable devastation, dissolving the target into its constituent atoms, sending bone-charring arcs of living lightning rippling through the enemy ranks, or phasing in and out of reality to bypass armour.

## RANGED WEAPONS

| WEAPON | RANGE | TYPE | S | AP | D | ABILITIES |
|---|---|---|---|---|---|---|
| Death ray | 24" | Heavy D3 | 10 | -4 | D6 | - |
| Doomsday cannon | | When attacking with this weapon, choose one of the profiles below. | | | | |
| - Low power | 36" | Heavy D6 | 8 | -2 | D3 | - |
| - High power | 72" | Heavy D6 | 10 | -5 | D6 | A model can only fire the doomsday cannon at high power if it remained stationary in its preceding Movement phase. |
| Eldritch Lance (shooting) | 36" | Assault 1 | 8 | -4 | D6 | - |
| Gauntlet of fire | 8" | Assault D6 | 4 | 0 | 1 | This weapon automatically hits its target. |
| Gauss blaster | 24" | Rapid Fire 1 | 5 | -2 | 1 | - |
| Gauss cannon | 24" | Heavy 3 | 6 | -3 | D3 | - |
| Gauss flayer | 24" | Rapid Fire 1 | 4 | -1 | 1 | - |
| Gauss flayer array | 24" | Rapid Fire 5 | 4 | -1 | 1 | - |
| Gauss flux arc | 24" | Heavy 3 | 5 | -2 | 1 | - |
| Gaze of death | 12" | Assault D6 | * | -4 | D3 | This weapon wounds on a 2+, unless it is targeting a **VEHICLE** unit, in which case it wounds on a 6+. |
| Heat ray | | When attacking with this weapon, choose one of the profiles below. | | | | |
| - Dispersed | 8" | Heavy 2D6 | 5 | -1 | 1 | When you use this profile, this weapon automatically hits its target. |
| - Focused | 24" | Heavy 2 | 8 | -4 | D6 | When you use this profile, if the target is within half range, roll two dice when inflicting damage with it and discard the lowest result. |
| Heavy gauss cannon | 36" | Heavy 1 | 9 | -4 | D6 | - |
| Particle beamer | 24" | Assault 3 | 6 | 0 | 1 | - |
| Particle caster | 12" | Pistol 1 | 6 | 0 | 1 | - |
| Particle shredder | 24" | Heavy 6 | 7 | -1 | D3 | - |
| Particle whip | 24" | Heavy 6 | 8 | -2 | D3 | - |
| Rod of covenant (shooting) | 12" | Assault 1 | 5 | -3 | 1 | - |
| Staff of light (shooting) | 12" | Assault 3 | 5 | -2 | 1 | - |
| Staff of the Destroyer (shooting) | 18" | Assault 3 | 6 | -3 | 2 | - |
| Synaptic disintegrator | 24" | Rapid Fire 1 | 4 | 0 | 1 | This weapon may target a **CHARACTER** even if it is not the closest enemy unit. Each time you roll a wound roll of 6+ for this weapon, the target suffers a mortal wound in addition to any other damage. |
| Tachyon arrow | 120" | Assault 1 | 10 | -5 | D6 | This weapon can only be used once per battle. |
| Tesla cannon | 24" | Assault 3 | 6 | 0 | 1 | Each hit roll of 6+ with this weapon causes 3 hits instead of 1. |
| Tesla carbine | 24" | Assault 2 | 5 | 0 | 1 | Each hit roll of 6+ with this weapon causes 3 hits instead of 1. |
| Tesla destructor | 24" | Assault 4 | 7 | 0 | 1 | Each hit roll of 6+ with this weapon causes 3 hits instead of 1. |
| Tesla sphere | 24" | Assault 5 | 7 | 0 | 1 | Each hit roll of 6+ with this weapon causes 3 hits instead of 1. |
| Transdimensional beamer | 12" | Heavy D3 | 4 | -3 | 1 | Each time you roll a wound roll of 6+ for this weapon, the target suffers a mortal wound in addition to any other damage. |
| Twin heavy gauss cannon | 36" | Heavy 2 | 9 | -4 | D6 | - |
| Twin tesla destructor | 24" | Assault 8 | 7 | 0 | 1 | Each hit roll of 6+ with this weapon causes 3 hits instead of 1. |

## MELEE WEAPONS

| WEAPON | RANGE | TYPE | S | AP | D | ABILITIES |
|---|---|---|---|---|---|---|
| Automaton claws | Melee | Melee | User | -2 | D3 | - |
| Crackling tendrils | Melee | Melee | User | -4 | D6 | - |
| Eldritch Lance (melee) | Melee | Melee | User | -2 | 1 | - |
| Empathic Obliterator | Melee | Melee | +2 | -1 | D3 | If a **CHARACTER** is slain by an attack from this weapon, each enemy unit within 6" of the slain character suffers D3 mortal wounds. |
| Feeder mandibles | Melee | Melee | User | 0 | 1 | If the target's Toughness is higher than this attack's Strength, this weapon always wounds the target on a wound roll of 5+. |
| Flayer claws | Melee | Melee | User | 0 | 1 | You can re-roll failed wound rolls for this weapon. |
| Hyperphase sword | Melee | Melee | +1 | -3 | 1 | - |
| Massive forelimbs | Melee | Melee | User | -1 | D3 | - |
| Rod of covenant (melee) | Melee | Melee | User | -3 | 1 | - |
| Scythe of the Nightbringer | Melee | Melee | * | -4 | D6 | This weapon wounds on a 2+, unless it is targeting a **VEHICLE** unit, in which case it has a Strength characteristic of 7. |
| Staff of light (melee) | Melee | Melee | User | -2 | 1 | - |
| Staff of the Destroyer (melee) | Melee | Melee | +1 | -3 | 2 | - |
| Staff of Tomorrow | Melee | Melee | User | -3 | D3 | You can re-roll failed hit rolls for this weapon. |
| Star-god fists | Melee | Melee | User | -4 | 3 | - |
| Vicious claws | Melee | Melee | User | -2 | 2 | - |
| Voidblade | Melee | Melee | User | -3 | 1 | Each time the bearer fights, it can make 1 additional attack with this weapon. |
| Voidscythe | Melee | Melee | x2 | -4 | 3 | When attacking with this weapon, subtract 1 from the hit roll. |
| Warscythe | Melee | Melee | +2 | -4 | 2 | - |
| Whip coils | Melee | Melee | User | -2 | 2 | If the bearer is slain in the Fight phase before it has made its attacks, leave the model where it is. When its unit is chosen to fight in that phase, it can do so as normal. Once it has done so, remove the model from the battlefield. |

## OTHER WARGEAR

| WARGEAR | ABILITIES |
|---|---|
| Canoptek cloak | A model equipped with a Canoptek cloak has a Move characteristic of 10" and gains the **FLY** keyword. In addition, at the start of your turn you can select one friendly <**DYNASTY**> model that has the Living Metal ability and that is within 3" of this model. That model regains D3 lost wounds, rather than 1, from its Living Metal ability. |
| Chronometron | <**DYNASTY**> **INFANTRY** units within 3" of a friendly <**DYNASTY**> model with a chronometron have a 5+ invulnerable save against ranged weapons. |
| Phylactery | A model with a phylactery regains D3 lost wounds at the beginning of your turn, rather than 1, from their Living Metal ability. |
| Resurrection orb | If a model has a resurrection orb, once per battle, immediately after you have made your Reanimation Protocols rolls at the beginning of the turn, you can make Reanimation Protocols rolls for models from a friendly <**DYNASTY**> **INFANTRY** unit within 3" of that model. |

In their relentless search for relics of the Machine God, the servants of the Adeptus Mechanicus have encroached upon the rightful domain of the Necrons of the Sautekh Dynasty. Commanded by their ancient tyrant-kings, these soulless creatures of living metal

# CODE OF WAR

In this section you'll find rules for Battle-forged armies that include NECRONS Detachments – that is, any Detachment which includes only NECRONS units. These rules include the abilities below and a series of Stratagems that can only be used by the Necrons. This section also includes the Necrons' unique Warlord Traits, Powers of the C'tan, Relics and Tactical Objectives. Together, these rules reflect the character and fighting style of the Necrons in your games of Warhammer 40,000.

## ABILITIES

All NECRONS Detachments (excluding Super-heavy Auxiliary Detachments) gain the following abilities:

### THEIR NUMBER IS LEGION, THEIR NAME IS DEATH

*The Necron dynasties are assured in their supremacy, for the galaxy was once theirs and will be again. All shall kneel before the might of the phaerons or be destroyed.*

If your army is Battle-forged, all Troops units in NECRONS Detachments gain this ability. Such a unit that is within range of an objective marker (as specified in the mission) controls that objective marker even if there are more enemy models within range of it. If an enemy unit within range of the same objective marker has a similar ability, then the objective marker is controlled by the player who has the most models within range of it as normal.

## DYNASTIC CODES

*The scattered dynasties of the Necrontyr pursue many different paths to dominance, embracing their own traditions, arcane technologies and martial doctrines.*

If your army is Battle-forged, units with the appropriate keyword will receive the corresponding Dynastic Code, detailed opposite, so long as every other unit in their Detachment is from the same dynasty (with the exception of those listed below). If you have chosen a dynasty that does not feature on this list, you can choose the Dynastic Code that best suits the fighting style and battlefield strategies of the warriors that hail from it.

## Dynastic Agents and Star Gods

The units listed below can be included in a NECRONS Detachment without preventing other units in that Detachment from gaining a Dynastic Code. Note, however, that the units listed below can never themselves benefit from a Dynastic Code.

- Anrakyr the Traveller
- Illuminor Szeras
- Triarch Praetorians
- Triarch Stalkers
- C'TAN SHARD units

# DYNASTIC CODES

## SAUTEKH:
### RELENTLESS ADVANCE

*Nothing can halt the inexorable march of the Sautekh. These disdainful conquerors will stop at nothing to retake their ancient domain, obliterating any who dare defy them in a storm of death and destruction.*

If a unit with this code Advances, it treats all ranged weapons it is equipped with as Assault weapons until the end of the turn (e.g. a Rapid Fire 1 weapon is treated as an Assault 1 weapon, and a Heavy D6 weapon is treated as an Assault D6 weapon etc.). In addition, unless it has Advanced this turn, a unit with this code does not suffer the penalty to hit rolls for moving and firing a Heavy weapon.

## MEPHRIT:
### SOLAR FURY

*The Mephrit have harnessed the power of captive suns to power their weapons. This raging solar energy can sear through even the thickest armour with ease.*

Each time a model with this code shoots an enemy unit that is within half range of its weapon's maximum range, the Armour Penetration characteristic of that weapon's attack is improved by 1 (i.e. an Armour Penetration characteristic of '0' becomes '-1', an Armour Penetration characteristic of '-1' becomes '-2', etc.).

## NOVOKH:
### AWAKENED BY MURDER

*The crimson hosts of Novokh remember well the sacred rites of blooding performed by their warriors in the ancient times. The dynasty's proud martial heritage awakens a spark of violent pride within its legions, lending power and ferocity to their attacks.*

You can re-roll failed hit rolls in the Fight phase for units with this code if they charged, were charged, or performed a Heroic Intervention this turn.

## NIHILAKH:
### AGGRESSIVELY TERRITORIAL

*Regal and arrogant, the warriors of this proud dynasty will not give a single inch to their foes. They stand their ground defiantly, unleashing a formidably accurate hail of fire that cleanses the stain of the lesser races from their rightful lands.*

Re-roll hit rolls of 1 for units with this code whenever they shoot, including when firing Overwatch, as long as they did not move in the preceding Movement phase and they have not disembarked from a **TRANSPORT** during this turn.

## NEPHREKH:
### TRANSLOCATION BEAMS

*The bodies of the Nephrekh are crafted from metagold. This rare and wondrous alloy allows them to transform into beams of pure light in order to teleport across open ground and even phase through solid matter.*

If a unit with this code Advances, add 6" to its Move characteristic for that Movement phase instead of rolling a dice (if the unit is being affected by the My Will Be Done or Wave of Command ability, add 7" to its Move characteristic instead). In addition, if a unit with this code Advances, its models can move across models and terrain as if they were not there.

# STRATAGEMS

If your army is Battle-forged and includes any Necrons Detachments (excluding Auxiliary Support Detachments), you have access to the Stratagems shown here, meaning you can spend Command Points to activate them. These help to reflect the unique strategies used by the Necrons on the battlefield.

## ENHANCED REANIMATION PROTOCOLS
**2CP**

*Necrons Stratagem*

*The Necrons are a deathless foe that can recover from obliteration time and again.*

Use this Stratagem before making Reanimation Protocols rolls for a unit from your army. You can re-roll Reanimation Protocols rolls of 1 for that unit this turn.

## WRATH OF THE C'TAN
**2CP**

*Necrons Stratagem*

*The C'tan's ever-burning rage at their enslavement is turned upon the enemy with cataclysmic results.*

Use this Stratagem after a C'tan Shard from your army has resolved a Power of the C'tan. Roll a D6 to randomly select a Power of the C'tan from page 113. The C'tan Shard immediately uses the power rolled, even if it has already used that power this phase.

## EMERGENCY INVASION BEAM
**1CP**

*Necrons Stratagem*

*Before it is destroyed, the Necron construct shifts all power to its dimensional gateway, beaming in warriors to take its place.*

Use this Stratagem when the last <Dynasty> Night Scythe and/or Monolith from your army is destroyed. Before removing the model from the battlefield, you can immediately set up a friendly <Dynasty> unit still on their tomb world wholly within 3" of the Night Scythe/Monolith and more than 1" from any enemy models.

## AMALGAMATED TARGETING DATA
**1CP**

*Necrons Stratagem*

*Synchronised targeting optics are fed to the Doom Scythe squadron, and they release a devastating pinpoint barrage.*

Use this Stratagem in your Shooting phase if a <Dynasty> Doom Scythe from your army is within 6" of 2 other friendly <Dynasty> Doom Scythes. The Doom Scythes cannot fire their death rays this phase – instead, select a point on the battlefield within 24" of all three vehicles that is visible to all of them. Roll a D6 for each unit within 3" of that point. Add 1 to the result if the unit being rolled for has 5 or more models, but subtract 1 if the unit being rolled for is a Character. On a 4+, that unit suffers 3D3 mortal wounds.

## DYNASTIC HEIRLOOMS
**1CP/3CP**

*Necrons Stratagem*

*In times of need, the phaerons will order the relic-vaults emptied, their priceless contents distributed amongst the legions.*

Use this Stratagem before the battle. Your army can have one extra Artefact of the Aeons for 1 CP, or two extra Artefacts of the Aeons for 3 CPs. All of the Artefacts of the Aeons that you include must be different and be given to different Necrons Characters. This Stratagem can only be used once per battle.

## ENHANCED INVASION BEAM
**1CP**

*Necrons Stratagem*

*A shimmering dimensional portal yawns wide for a few moments, spilling yet more fleshless warriors into the fray.*

Use this Stratagem before you set up a unit from a tomb world using the Invasion Beams ability of a Night Scythe from your army, or the Eternity Gate ability of a Monolith from your army. You can set up two units from a tomb world instead of one.

## SOLAR PULSE
**1CP**

*Necrons Stratagem*

*Many Necron weapons contain pulsing orbs within which is bound the awesome power of a solar flare.*

Use this Stratagem after a Necrons unit from your army has declared its targets in the Shooting phase, but before any hit rolls are made. Pick one of the enemy units that your unit is targeting. The enemy unit does not receive the benefit of cover against your unit's weapons this phase.

## RESURRECTION PROTOCOLS
**1CP**

*Necrons Stratagem*

*Necron rulers possess sophisticated self-repair systems that can knit together even the most grievous wounds.*

Use this Stratagem when a Necrons Character from your army (excluding Trazyn the Infinite and C'tan Shards) is slain. At the end of that phase, roll a D6. On a 4+ set the character up again, as close as possible to his previous position, and more than 1" from any enemy models, with 1 wound remaining. This Stratagem cannot be used to resurrect the same model more than once per battle.

## DAMAGE CONTROL OVERRIDE
**1CP**

*Necrons Stratagem*

*Its self-repair routines overridden, the vehicle briefly operates at peak efficiency despite being critically damaged.*

Use this Stratagem at the start of any turn. Pick a **NECRONS VEHICLE** from your army. Until the end of this turn, use the top row of that vehicle's damage table, regardless of how many wounds it has left. This ends immediately if the model is reduced to 0 wounds.

## REPAIR SUBROUTINES
**2CP**

*Necrons Stratagem*

*When engaged in a battle of attrition, Canoptek constructs react by enabling a series of repairing adaptive subroutines.*

Use this Stratagem at the start of your turn, before making any Reanimation Protocols rolls. Select a **CANOPTEK** unit from your army that is on the battlefield. That unit gains the Reanimation Protocols ability until the end of your turn.

## SELF-DESTRUCTION
**1CP**

*Necrons Stratagem*

*The self-destruct protocols of Canoptek Scarabs cause them to explode in a hail of razor-sharp armour fragments.*

Use this Stratagem after a unit of Canoptek Scarabs from your army piles in, but before they make their close combat attacks. Select a Canoptek Scarab Swarm model in your unit and then pick an enemy unit within 1" of it. Your Canoptek Scarab Swarm model is destroyed. Remove it from the battlefield and roll a D6; on a 2+ the enemy unit you picked suffers D3 mortal wounds.

## DISRUPTION FIELDS
**1CP**

*Necrons Stratagem*

*The thrumming aura of negative energy known as a disruption field warps and dissolves both armour and flesh.*

Use this Stratagem before a **NECRONS INFANTRY** unit from your army fights in the Fight phase. Increase the Strength characteristic of all models in that unit by 1 until the end of the phase.

## ENTROPIC STRIKE
**1CP**

*Necrons Stratagem*

*The disruption field emanating from this warrior's weapon is so powerful that it entirely obliterates matter from existence.*

Use this Stratagem in the Fight phase before a **NECRONS CHARACTER** from your army fights. Invulnerable saves cannot be taken against the first close combat attack made by this character this phase.

## DISPERSION FIELD AMPLIFICATION
**2CP**

*Necrons Stratagem*

*Lychguard can overcharge the fields of their dispersion shields.*

Use this Stratagem in the Shooting phase when an enemy unit targets a unit of Lychguard from your army equipped with dispersion shields. Your unit's invulnerable save is improved to 3+ until the end of the phase. In addition, until the end of the phase, each time you roll an unmodified 6 for this unit's invulnerable saving throw, the unit that made that attack suffers a mortal wound after it has finished making all of its shooting attacks.

## QUANTUM DEFLECTION
**1CP**

*Necrons Stratagem*

*Necron quantum shielding is a true marvel of techno-arcana, phasing into existence only at the moment of impact.*

Use this Stratagem when an enemy unit targets a **VEHICLE** in your army that has the Quantum Shielding ability, but before any hit rolls are made. Until the end of the phase, subtract 1 from rolls made for your vehicle's Quantum Shielding ability to see if damage is ignored for each unsaved wound.

## EXTERMINATION PROTOCOLS
**1CP**

*Necrons Stratagem*

*Destroyers have sacrificed every last ember of their souls in order to pursue the obliteration of all mortal life.*

Use this Stratagem in your Shooting phase before shooting with a Destroyer Lord, a unit of Destroyers or a unit of Heavy Destroyers from your army. Re-roll failed hit and wound rolls for that unit until the end of the phase.

## THE PHAERON'S WILL
**1CP**

*Necrons Stratagem*

*The generals of the Necron Empire are peerless strategists who have overseen the obliteration of countless civilisations.*

Use this Stratagem after an **OVERLORD** from your army has used their My Will Be Done or Wave of Command ability. That model can immediately use that ability for a second time this turn.

## ADAPTIVE SUBROUTINES
**1CP**

*Necrons Stratagem*

*The Crypteks have invested their mechanical constructs with complex hunter-killer algorithms.*

Use this Stratagem after a **CANOPTEK** unit from your army has Advanced. That unit can still shoot and/or charge this turn.

## DIMENSIONAL CORRIDOR

**1CP**

*Necrons Stratagem*

*Necron Monoliths can redirect a tomb world's forces by projecting a series of short-ranged dimensional portals.*

Use this Stratagem at the start of your Movement phase. Select a <DYNASTY> INFANTRY unit from your army that is more than 1" from any enemy models and remove it from the battlefield. Then, set the unit up again so that it is wholly within 3" of a <DYNASTY> Monolith from your army and more than 1" from any enemy models. That unit counts as having disembarked from the Monolith this turn and can move normally.

## JUDGEMENT OF THE TRIARCH

**1CP**

*Necrons Stratagem*

*Those who defy the will of the Triarch are subject to swift and merciless retribution.*

Use this Stratagem before a unit of Triarch Praetorians from your army shoots in the Shooting phase or fights in the Fight phase. Add 1 to hit rolls made for this unit until the end of the phase.

## GRAVITIC SINGULARITY

**1CP**

*Necrons Stratagem*

*A pulsing gravitic anomaly appears in the sky over the Obelisk, dragging enemy aircraft into its crushing embrace.*

Use this Stratagem at the start of your Shooting phase. Select an Obelisk from your army. When resolving this model's Gravity Pulse ability this phase, each enemy unit within range that can FLY suffers D3 mortal wounds on a roll of 4+, instead of a roll of 6.

## COSMIC POWERS

**1CP**

*Necrons Stratagem*

*The powers of the C'tan are myriad and terrifying. To battle a fragment of these shackled star gods is to find reality unbound.*

Use this Stratagem at the start of your Movement phase. Select a C'TAN SHARD from your army. That model can replace one of its Powers of the C'tan with a different Power of the C'tan of your choice.

*'I have seen the death of stars, mortal. I have seen the gods themselves bowed and broken, enslaved to the whims of the empire. And you think to resist?'*

*- Overlord Lacras of the Mephrit Dynasty*

## METHODICAL DESTRUCTION

**2CP**

*Sautekh Stratagem*

*The Sautekh Dynasty excel in systematic killing, marking each target until it is completely obliterated.*

Use this Stratagem after a SAUTEKH unit from your army has inflicted an unsaved wound on an enemy unit. Add 1 to hit rolls for friendly SAUTEKH units that target the same enemy unit this phase.

## RECLAIM A LOST EMPIRE

**2CP**

*Nihilakh Stratagem*

*The Nihilakh seek to rule the galaxy, and once they have claimed a domain it is almost impossible to drive them from it.*

Use this Stratagem at the end of your turn. Select a NIHILAKH unit from your army. If the unit is within 3" of an objective marker, or if it did not move for any reason during its turn, then until the start of your next turn you can add 1 to saving throws made for that unit and increase the Attacks characteristic of models in that unit by 1.

## TRANSLOCATION CRYPT

**1CP**

*Nephrekh Stratagem*

*Masters of teleportation technology, the Nephrekh ride into battle upon blinding beams of light.*

Use this Stratagem during deployment. You can set up a NEPHREKH INFANTRY or SWARM unit from your army in a translocation crypt instead of placing it on the battlefield. At the end of any of your Movement phases this unit can translocate into battle – set it up anywhere on the battlefield that is more than 9" away from any enemy models.

## BLOOD RITES

**3CP**

*Novokh Stratagem*

*Novokh's warriors have mastered the arts of martial warfare, and their deathless bodies allow them to fight on tirelessly.*

Use this Stratagem at the end of the Fight phase. Select a NOVOKH unit from your army – that unit can immediately fight for a second time.

## TALENT FOR ANNIHILATION

**1CP**

*Mephrit Stratagem*

*The Mephrit seek not merely to defeat their foes, but to entirely expunge them from the face of the galaxy.*

Use this Stratagem before a MEPHRIT unit from your army attacks in the Shooting phase. Each time you make an unmodified hit roll of 6 for a model in that unit, you can make one additional hit roll for that model with the same weapon against the same target. These additional hit rolls cannot themselves generate any further hit rolls.

# POWERS OF THE C'TAN

To the shards of the C'tan, reality is merely another weapon to be turned against their foes. It is within the prodigious powers of the god-fragments to summon forth storms of annihilating negative matter, shatter the foundation of a planet, or cast their enemies out of existence with but a thought.

Before the battle, generate Powers of the C'tan for each **C'TAN SHARD** unit using the table below. Roll a D6 to generate their powers randomly (re-rolling any duplicate results). Before the battle, you can instead choose the powers each of these units have, but if you do this you cannot choose a power for a second time until all six have been chosen once each (similarly, you cannot choose a power for a third time until all six have been chosen twice each, and so on).

## D6 RESULT

### 1 ANTIMATTER METEOR

*The C'tan Shard gathers an orb of roiling antimatter, before hurling the crackling projectile into the midst of the foe.*

Roll a D6. On a 2+ the closest visible enemy unit within 24" of the C'tan Shard suffers D3 mortal wounds. On a 6, it suffers D6 mortal wounds instead. If the C'tan Shard using this power is a Tesseract Vault, the unit suffers D6 mortal wounds on the roll of a 5+ instead.

### 2 TIME'S ARROW

*Mutating the flow of causality and remoulding the temporal streams, the C'tan Shard erases its foe's very existence from space and time.*

Pick a visible enemy unit within 18" of the C'tan Shard and roll a D6, adding 1 to the result if the C'tan Shard using this power is a Tesseract Vault. If the result exceeds the highest Wounds characteristic in the unit, one model from that unit, chosen by the controlling player, is slain. An unmodified roll of 1 will always fail.

### 3 SKY OF FALLING STARS

*Savagely beautiful orbs of coruscating light plummet from the cold depths of space, growing to roaring bale-stars as they approach.*

Pick up to three different enemy units that are within 18" of the C'tan Shard. Roll a D6 for each, subtracting 1 from the result if the C'tan Shard using this power is a Tesseract Vault. If the result is less than the number of models in that unit, the unit suffers D3 mortal wounds. An unmodified roll of 6 will always fail.

### 4 COSMIC FIRE

*At the C'tan Shard's gestured command, a pillar of black fire streaks down from the heavens to consume the foe.*

Roll a D6 for each enemy unit within 9" of the C'tan Shard. Add 1 to the roll if the C'tan Shard using this power is a Tesseract Vault. On a 4+ the unit being rolled for suffers D3 mortal wounds.

### 5 SEISMIC ASSAULT

*Stone fractures and ores melt as the C'tan Shard drags up tides of magma from deep below.*

Pick a visible enemy unit within 24" of the C'tan Shard and roll a D6 for each model in that unit. Add 1 to the roll if the C'tan Shard using this power is a Tesseract Vault. For each result of 6+ that unit suffers a mortal wound.

### 6 TRANSDIMENSIONAL THUNDERBOLT

*The C'tan Shard projects a crackling bolt of energy from its outstretched palm, blasting its foe into oblivion.*

Pick a visible enemy unit within 24" of the C'tan Shard and roll a D6 (you can only pick a **CHARACTER** if it has 10 or more Wounds and/or it is the closest enemy model to the C'tan Shard). Add 1 to the result if the C'tan Shard using this power is a Tesseract Vault. On a 4+ the chosen unit suffers D3 mortal wounds. Then, roll a D6 for every other enemy unit that is within 3" of the chosen enemy unit. On a 4+ the unit being rolled for suffers a mortal wound.

'We must not let the relics of antiquity be broken and crushed by the savagery of unenlightened creatures, for only by understanding these treasures may we conquer the future. Only we, who have broken free from the shackles of mortality and bound the infinite majesty of the cosmos to our will, can be trusted with this task. That is why we are here, on this wretched pit of a planet. Eliminate these mortals as you see fit, but do try to keep the collateral damage to a minimum.'

- *Trazyn the Infinite*

# ARTEFACTS OF THE AEONS

he vaults of the Necron Dynasties contain all manner of esoteric artefact, forged long before many of the lesser races even xisted. These relics possess star-shattering power, and are granted only to the greatest lords of the empire, who turn them owards the complete obliteration of their enemies.

your army is led by a **NECRONS** Warlord, then before the battle ou may give one of the following Artefacts of the Aeons to a **ECRONS CHARACTER** (excluding **C'TAN SHARDS**). Named haracters such as Imotekh the Stormlord already have one or ore artefacts and cannot be given any of the following artefacts.

ote that some weapons replace one of the character's existing eapons or items of wargear. Where this is the case, if you are aying a matched play game or are otherwise using points values, ou must still pay the cost of the weapon or item of wargear that being replaced. Write down any Artefacts of the Aeons your haracters have on your army roster.

## HE ORB OF ETERNITY

*ie Orb of Eternity is thought to be the first resurrection orb ever eated. For millennia, it rested in a primitive fane on the world of rmandus, where the indigenous populace marvelled at its seemingly vine ability to effect repairs upon their technologies. Ever since this ate of affairs was righted by a host of Triarch Praetorians, the orb is iparted as a boon to those nobles who are deemed worthy.*

odel with resurrection orb only. The Orb of Eternity replaces the arer's resurrection orb. If a model has the Orb of Eternity, once er battle, immediately after you have made your Reanimation rotocols rolls, you can make Reanimation Protocols rolls for odels from a friendly <**DYNASTY**> **INFANTRY** unit within 3" of the arer; when making these rolls add 1 to the result of each roll.

## OIDREAPER

*egend has it that on the day Aza'gorod the Nightbringer was ndered into shards, this warscythe appeared in the armoury of the ekthyst Dynasty's crownworld. Its blade is a sliver of the void, and hen swung, it cuts through more than just mere physical forms. Its ctims drop to the ground as husks, their souls torn from their bodies e tattered shrouds before dissipating with final screams of horror.*

lodel with warscythe or voidscythe only. Voidreaper replaces the arer's warscythe or voidscythe and has the following profile:

| WEAPON | RANGE | TYPE | S | AP | D |
|---|---|---|---|---|---|
| Voidreaper | Melee | Melee | * | -4 | 3 |

**Abilities:** This weapon wounds on a 2+, unless it is targeting a **VEHICLE** unit, n which case it has a Strength of 7.

## GHTNING FIELD

*his formidable adaptation of tesla weapon technology is a defensive ield that surrounds the bearer with a web of emerald lightning. Any e that attempts to draw close is engulfed in this living electricity, id swiftly transformed into a blackened, smoking skeleton.*

he bearer of the Lightning Field has a 4+ invulnerable save. In ddition, roll a D6 for each enemy unit that is within 1" of the arer at the start of the Fight phase. On a 4+ that unit suffers a ortal wound.

## THE NIGHTMARE SHROUD

*This heavy cloak of living-metal scales was forged by Ut-Hekneth the Unsleeping during his million-year madness. The cloak itself is virtually indestructible, each scale formed from quantum-folded layers of void-hardened adamantium bonded with a hyper-flexible energy weave. This is a by-product of its primary design however, which is to project the worst excesses of Ut-Hekneth's madness, assailing nearby enemies with phantasms of dread as potent as any mortal danger.*

The bearer's Save characteristic is improved by 1 (i.e. a Save characteristic of 4+ becomes 3+, a Save characteristic of 3+ becomes 2+ etc.). In addition, enemy units subtract 1 from their Leadership characteristic whilst they are within 6" of the bearer of the Nightmare Shroud.

## THE GAUNTLET OF THE CONFLAGRATOR

*Crafted by the Cryptek Harri'apt the Conflagrator, this gauntlet uses interdimensional energy-exchangers to open a microscopic conduit to the raging heart of a star. The superheated plasmic flame that erupts through this hole is forced down a cone of hyperdense gravitons that spew the energy forth in a blazing cloud of unstoppable fury.*

The Gauntlet of the Conflagrator has the following profile:

| WEAPON | RANGE | TYPE | S | AP | D |
|---|---|---|---|---|---|
| Gauntlet of the Conflagrator | 8" | Pistol 1 | - | - | - |

**Abilities:** This weapon can only be fired once per battle. This weapon automatically hits its target; roll one D6 for each model in the target unit that is within 8" of the firer – that unit suffers a mortal wound for each roll of 6.

## THE VEIL OF DARKNESS

*This device was fashioned from transpositanium, a substance so rare that it can only be found in a handful of places in the galaxy. It is highly sought after by the Necrons, and wars have been waged to secure it. Activated with a thought, the veil causes space and time to warp around its user and those near them, enfolding them in a swirling darkness. As the darkness fades, the user and their comrades appear elsewhere on the battlefield, transported through a miracle of arcane science.*

Once per battle, at the end of any of your Movement phases, the bearer can use the Veil of Darkness. When they do, the bearer, and up to one friendly <**DYNASTY**> **INFANTRY** unit within 3" of the bearer, are removed from the battlefield. Then, set up the bearer (and the second unit you chose, if any) anywhere on the battlefield that is more than 9" from any enemy models (the second unit mus be set up wholly within 6" of the bearer).

## THE NANOSCARAB CASKET

*Invented by the Cryptek scientist known as the Onyx Swarm, this unassuming vial of black crystal is filled with thousands of tiny writhing Canoptek automatons. Once released, the swarm of miniaturised constructs envelops the bearer's necrodermis, repairing grievous wounds and flooding their body with synthetic stimuli.*

Model with phylactery only. The Nanoscarab Casket replaces the bearer's phylactery. The bearer of the Nanoscarab Casket regains D3 lost wounds at the beginning of your turn, rather than 1, from their Living Metal ability. In addition, the bearer also regains D3 lost wounds at the beginning of your opponent's turn. The first time the bearer is slain, roll a D6. On a 4+ set the bearer up again at the end of the phase, as close as possible to its previous position, and more than 1" from any enemy models, with D6 wounds remaining.

## SEMPITERNAL WEAVE

*Only the finest Cryptek artificers know the secret of crafting a Sempiternal Weave. These gossamer-thin plates are formed from phase-hardened amarathine and threads of adamantium. They are then layered over the bearer's carapace of living metal, and when struck they stiffen and contract, turning aside energy blades, bolt shells and even the searing heat of a plasma burst.*

INFANTRY model only. Increase the Toughness and Wounds characteristics of the bearer by 1.

## THE ABYSSAL STAFF

*To succumb to the swirling ebon mist called forth from an abyssal staff is to be swallowed by impenetrable madness. Legend has it that Sautekh Crypteks have embedded each of these artefacts with a tiny sliver from the necrodermis of the Deceiver, allowing the bearer to summon wisps of shadow imbued with the star god's anarchic insanity. These emanations drive victims to tear at their flesh and gouge out their eyes, gibber uncontrollably, or open fire on their allies.*

SAUTEKH model with staff of light only. The Abyssal Staff replaces the bearer's staff of light and has the following profile:

| WEAPON | RANGE | TYPE | S | AP | D |
|---|---|---|---|---|---|
| The Abyssal Staff (shooting) | 12" | Assault 1 | * | * | * |
| The Abyssal Staff (melee) | Melee | Melee | User | -2 | 1 |

**Abilities:** This weapon automatically hits its target. Roll 3D6 if a unit is hit by this weapon in the Shooting phase; if the result is equal to or greater than the target unit's highest Leadership characteristic, then it suffers D3 mortal wounds.

## TIMESPLINTER CLOAK

*Fashioned by the chronomancers of the Nihilakh Dynasty, this relic grants the bearer the ability to alter their destiny. This glittering shroud is formed from slivers of crystallised time, and the bearer can expend the power of these shards to glimpse a matrix of potential futures. The knowledge granted by this foresight allows them to perform incredible feats in battle.*

NIHILAKH model only. Once per battle, you can re-roll a single hit roll, wound roll or damage roll made for the bearer of the Timesplinter Cloak. In addition, roll a dice each time the bearer loses a wound; on a 5+, the model does not lose that wound.

## THE VOLTAIC STAFF

*The Mephrit are masters of the art of aethermancy, and the greatest of their creations is the Voltaic Staff. Blazing arcs of lightning continuously ripple down the shaft of this onyx stave, and the bearer can send these electrostatic beams hurtling towards his enemies with fearsome rapidity. Living targets are enveloped in a searing halo of bone-charring voltage, while vehicles find their guidance systems burned out and their hulls peeled open.*

MEPHRIT model with staff of light only. The Voltaic Staff replaces the bearer's staff of light and has the following profile:

| WEAPON | RANGE | TYPE | S | AP | D |
|---|---|---|---|---|---|
| The Voltaic Staff (shooting) | 12" | Assault 3 | 6 | -3 | 2 |
| The Voltaic Staff (melee) | Melee | Melee | User | -2 | 1 |

**Abilities:** Each time you make a wound roll of 6+ for this weapon in the Shooting phase, the target suffers a mortal wound in addition to any other damage.

## THE BLOOD SCYTHE

*It is said that Ultep the Divider fought ten thousand duels, and was never once defeated. He is amongst the greatest heroes of the Novokh, venerated to this day by the dynasty's warrior cults. Only the untrammelled power of a rampaging C'tan finally scattered Ultep's metal body to atoms, though his crimson war scythe survived his destruction. Forged from sanguiphagic starmetal alloys, a single cut from this blade can siphon a torrent of blood from an opponent.*

NOVOKH model with warscythe or voidscythe only. The Blood Scythe replaces the bearer's warscythe or voidscythe and has the following profile:

| WEAPON | RANGE | TYPE | S | AP | D |
|---|---|---|---|---|---|
| Blood Scythe | Melee | Melee | +2 | -4 | 2 |

**Abilities:** Each time the bearer fights, it can make D3 additional attacks with this weapon.

## THE SOLAR STAFF

*Forged within the Heliaconvarium of Aryand, the Solar Staff burns with the light of truth and honour. Set loose, the staff's energies blaze outward in a mighty flare, as though a new sun was born. The darkness is driven back by this false dawn, and the foe reels as their eyes are blinded and their deceptions are laid bare.*

NEPHREKH model with staff of light only. The Solar Staff replaces the bearer's staff of light and has the following profile:

| WEAPON | RANGE | TYPE | S | AP | D |
|---|---|---|---|---|---|
| The Solar Staff (shooting) | 12" | Assault 6 | 5 | -3 | 1 |
| The Solar Staff (melee) | Melee | Melee | User | -2 | 1 |

**Abilities:** Each time an enemy INFANTRY unit is hit by this weapon in the Shooting phase, roll a D6; on a 4+ the enemy unit is blinded until the end of the turn – it cannot fire Overwatch and your opponent must subtract 1 from any hit rolls made for the unit.

# WARLORD TRAITS

The rulers of the Necron Empire have waged war across the stars for millennia, bending stellar domains and proud kingdoms to their will, shattering armies and crushing all who would oppose them. These formidable strategists share an unquenchable desire for conquest and domination, though the great lords of each dynasty adhere to their own martial traditions and warrior codes.

If a NECRONS CHARACTER is your Warlord, he can generate a Warlord Trait from the following table instead of the one in the *Warhammer 40,000* rulebook. You can either roll on the table below to randomly generate a Warlord Trait, or you can select the one that best suits his temperament and preferred style of waging war.

## D6 RESULT

### 1 ENDURING WILL
*This Warlord is possessed of iron resolve, and no mortal weaponry will prevent him from achieving his goals.*

Reduce any damage inflicted on your Warlord by 1 (to a minimum of 1). For example, if your Warlord fails a saving throw against an attack that inflicts 3 damage, they will only lose 2 wounds.

### 2 ETERNAL MADNESS
*This Warlord's sanity suffered during the Great Sleep, and now he is driven by a wrathful zeal.*

You can re-roll failed wound rolls for your Warlord in the Fight phase if he charged, was charged, or performed a Heroic Intervention this turn.

### 3 IMMORTAL PRIDE
*This Warlord possesses an arrogance that has been honed over aeons, refusing to allow his warriors a single step backwards even in the face of intense psychic onslaught.*

Friendly <DYNASTY> units automatically pass Morale tests whilst they are within 6" of your Warlord. In addition, your Warlord can attempt to deny one psychic power in each enemy Psychic phase in the same manner as a PSYKER.

### 4 THRALL OF THE SILENT KING
*This Warlord pursues the veiled agenda of the Silent King, and so commands his legions with unparalleled authority.*

Increase the range of all abilities on your Warlord's datasheet by 3". If a Catacomb Command Barge has this Warlord Trait, this does not apply to its Explodes ability. If a Cryptek has this Warlord Trait, only increase the range of that model's Technomancer ability, not that of all other CRYPTEKS in your army. If a Cryptek with a Canoptek cloak has this Warlord Trait, this does not affect the distance the cloak allows the model to move in the Movement phase.

### 5 IMPLACABLE CONQUEROR
*This Warlord is a conqueror of worlds who strides at the head of his legions and sweeps away all before him.*

You can re-roll failed charge rolls for friendly <DYNASTY> units whilst they are within 6" of your Warlord.

### 6 HONOURABLE COMBATANT
*The Warlord is a strict adherent to the ancient codes of honour and sees a fight through to the end.*

If your Warlord targets the same enemy CHARACTER with all their close combat attacks, add D3 to your Warlord's Attacks characteristic until the end of the phase.

# DYNASTY WARLORD TRAITS

If you wish, you can pick a Dynasty Warlord Trait from the list below instead of using the Necrons Warlord Traits table, but only if your Warlord is from the relevant dynasty.

## Named Characters and Warlord Traits

If a named character is your Warlord, they must be given the associated Warlord Trait of their dynasty. For example, if Imotekh the Stormlord is your Warlord, he must have the Hyperlogical Strategist Warlord Trait, below. If Illuminor Szeras is your Warlord, he must have the Immortal Pride Warlord Trait, and if Anrakyr the Traveller is your Warlord, he must have the Implacable Conqueror Warlord Trait (see previous page).

| WARLORD | TRAIT |
|---------|-------|
| Sautekh | **Hyperlogical Strategist:** *Sautekh Warlords can apply a filter of infallible logic to develop unbeatable strategies.*<br><br>Once per battle, you can re-roll a single hit roll, wound roll or damage roll made for your Warlord. In addition, if your army is Battle-forged and your Warlord is on the battlefield, roll a D6 each time you spend a Command Point to use a Stratagem; on a 5+ that Command Point is immediately refunded. |
| Mephrit | **Merciless Tyrant:** *Warlords of Mephrit will suffer no threats to their rule, annihilating utterly any who dare to oppose them.*<br><br>Add 6" to the maximum range of all Assault weapons fired by your Warlord. In addition, your Warlord can shoot Assault weapons at enemy **Characters** even if they are not the closest enemy model. |
| Nihilakh | **Precognitive Strike:** *This Warlord of Nihilakh has foreseen his moment of glorious victory.*<br><br>Your Warlord always fights first in the Fight phase, even if he didn't charge. If your opponent has units that have charged, or that have a similar ability, then alternate choosing units to fight with, starting with the player whose turn is taking place. |
| Nephrekh | **Skin of Living Gold:** *This Nephrekh Warlord has ascended to become one with the stars themselves; those that gaze upon him are blinded by his radiant glory.*<br><br>Your opponent must subtract 1 from hit rolls that target your Warlord. |
| Novokh | **Crimson Haze:** *This Warlord leads his warriors in the bloody rituals of the Novokh.*<br><br>Each time you roll an unmodified hit roll of 6 in the Fight phase for a model in a friendly **Novokh** unit that is within 6" of your Warlord, you can make one additional hit roll for that model with the same weapon against the same target. These additional hit rolls cannot themselves generate any further hit rolls. |

'Spare me your condescension, human. You speak to a phaeron of the Infinite Empire. I was conquering the stars while your kind was wallowing in your own filth like witless beasts. Do not dare address me with such lack of respect again. Truce or no, I will see you buried in a lightless tomb with only the scarabs to hear your screams.'

- *Phaeron Thaszar the Invincible of the Sarnekh Dynasty, addressing Lord General Hausmann during the Hadrima Summit*

# POINTS VALUES

If you are playing a matched play game, or a game that uses a points limit, you can use the following lists to determine the total points cost of your army. Simply add together the points costs of all your models and the wargear they are equipped with to determine your army's total points value.

## NAMED CHARACTERS

| UNIT | MODELS PER UNIT | POINTS PER MODEL (Including wargear) |
|---|---|---|
| Anrakyr the Traveller | 1 | 167 |
| C'tan Shard of the Deceiver | 1 | 225 |
| C'tan Shard of the Nightbringer | 1 | 210 |
| Illuminor Szeras | 1 | 143 |
| Imotekh the Stormlord | 1 | 200 |
| Nemesor Zahndrekh | 1 | 180 |
| Orikan the Diviner | 1 | 115 |
| Trazyn the Infinite | 1 | 100 |
| Vargard Obyron | 1 | 140 |

## HQ UNITS

| UNIT | MODELS PER UNIT | POINTS PER MODEL (Does not include wargear) |
|---|---|---|
| Catacomb Command Barge | 1 | 138 |
| Cryptek | 1 | 70 |
| Destroyer Lord | 1 | 110 |
| Lord | 1 | 73 |
| Overlord | 1 | 84 |

## TROOPS

| UNIT | MODELS PER UNIT | POINTS PER MODEL (Does not include wargear) |
|---|---|---|
| Deathmarks | 5-10 | 19 |
| Immortals | 5-10 | 8 |
| Lychguard | 5-10 | 19 |
| Necron Warriors | 10-20 | 12 |

## ELITES

| UNIT | MODELS PER UNIT | POINTS PER MODEL (Does not include wargear) |
|---|---|---|
| Flayed Ones | 5-20 | 17 |
| Triarch Praetorians | 5-10 | 22 |
| Triarch Stalker | 1 | 117 |

## FAST ATTACK

| UNIT | MODELS PER UNIT | POINTS PER MODEL (Does not include wargear) |
|---|---|---|
| Canoptek Scarabs | 3-9 | 13 |
| Canoptek Wraiths | 3-6 | 55 |
| Destroyers | 1-6 | 30 |
| Tomb Blades | 3-9 | 14 |

## HEAVY SUPPORT

| UNIT | MODELS PER UNIT | POINTS PER MODEL (Does not include wargear) |
|---|---|---|
| Annihilation Barge | 1 | 133 |
| Canoptek Spyders | 1-3 | 65 |
| Doomsday Ark | 1 | 193 |
| Heavy Destroyers | 1-3 | 30 |
| Monolith | 1 | 381 |
| Transcendent C'tan | 1 | 225 |

## DEDICATED TRANSPORTS

| UNIT | MODELS PER UNIT | POINTS PER MODEL (Does not include wargear) |
|---|---|---|
| Ghost Ark | 1 | 160 |

## FLYERS

| UNIT | MODELS PER UNIT | POINTS PER MODEL (Does not include wargear) |
|---|---|---|
| Doom Scythe | 1 | 205 |
| Night Scythe | 1 | 160 |

## LORDS OF WAR

| UNIT | MODELS PER UNIT | POINTS PER MODEL (Does not include wargear) |
|---|---|---|
| Obelisk | 1 | 426 |
| Tesseract Vault | 1 | 496 |

## RANGED WEAPONS

| WEAPON | POINTS PER WEAPON |
|---|---|
| Death ray | 0 |
| Doomsday cannon | 0 |
| Gauss blaster | 9 |
| Gauss cannon | 20 |
| Gauss flayer | 0 |
| Gauss flayer array | 0 |
| Gauss flux arc | 0 |
| Heat ray | 54 |
| Heavy gauss cannon | 27 |
| Particle beamer | 10 |
| Particle caster | 4 |
| Particle shredder | 41 |
| Particle whip | 0 |
| Rod of covenant | 10 |
| Staff of light | 10 |
| Synaptic disintegrator | 0 |
| Tesla cannon | 13 |
| Tesla carbine | 9 |
| Tesla destructor | 0 |
| Tesla sphere | 0 |
| Transdimensional beamer | 14 |
| Twin heavy gauss cannon | 54 |
| Twin tesla destructor | 0 |

## MELEE WEAPONS

| WEAPON | POINTS PER WEAPON |
| --- | --- |
| Automaton claws | 0 |
| Crackling tendrils | 0 |
| Feeder mandibles | 0 |
| Flayer claws | 0 |
| Hyperphase sword | 3 |
| Massive forelimbs | 0 |
| Vicious claws | 0 |
| Voidblade | 6 |
| Voidscythe | 20 |
| Warscythe | 11 |
| Whip coils | 9 |

## OTHER WARGEAR

| WARGEAR | POINTS PER ITEM |
| --- | --- |
| Dispersion shield | 12 |
| Chronometron | 15 |
| Canoptek cloak | 5 |
| Fabricator claw array | 5 |
| Gloom prism | 5 |
| Nebuloscope | 2 |
| Phylactery | 10 |
| Resurrection orb | 35 |
| Shadowloom | 5 |
| Shieldvanes | 3 |

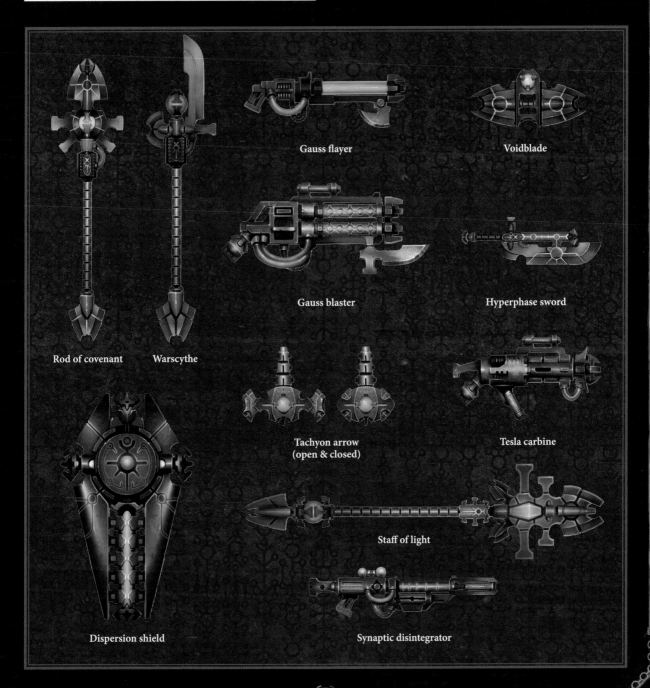

Rod of covenant

Warscythe

Gauss flayer

Gauss blaster

Voidblade

Hyperphase sword

Tachyon arrow
(open & closed)

Tesla carbine

Staff of light

Dispersion shield

Synaptic disintegrator

# TACTICAL OBJECTIVES

The ultimate goal of the Necrons is the total domination of the galaxy, and the subjugation or slaughter of the primitive races who dare to trespass upon their domain. The phaerons are utterly assured of their triumph, for their technology and martial strength have proven enough to enslave even gods to their will.

If your army is led by a **NECRONS** Warlord, these Tactical Objectives replace the Capture and Control Tactical Objectives (numbers 11-16) in the *Warhammer 40,000* rulebook. If a mission uses Tactical Objectives, players use the normal rules for using Tactical Objectives with the following exception: when a Necrons player generates a Capture and Control objective (numbers 11-16), they instead generate the corresponding Necrons Tactical Objective, as shown below. Other Tactical Objectives (numbers 21-66) are generated normally.

| D66 | TACTICAL OBJECTIVE |
|-----|--------------------|
| 11 | Endless Legions |
| 12 | Dust and Ashes |
| 13 | Reclaim and Recapture |
| 14 | Age of the Machine |
| 15 | Slaughter the Living |
| 16 | Code of Combat |

## 11 — ENDLESS LEGIONS *Necrons*

*The enemy cannot hope to win a war of attrition against you; watch the foe's joy at slaying your minions turn to dismay as the warriors of your legions reanimate before their eyes to continue the fight.*

Whilst this Tactical Objective is active, keep a tally of the total number of successful Reanimation Protocols rolls you make. Score 1 victory point if the tally reaches 10.

## 14 — AGE OF THE MACHINE *Necrons*

*The crude war machines of the lesser races are an affront to the technological supremacy of the Necrons. Exterminate them.*

Score 1 victory point if at least one enemy **VEHICLE** model was destroyed during this turn. If at least 3 enemy **VEHICLE** models were destroyed during this turn, score D3 victory points instead. If any of the destroyed vehicles was **TITANIC**, score an additional 3 victory points.

## 12 — DUST AND ASHES *Necrons*

*The Necrons have seen civilisations rise and fall and the stars burn themselves black. Some enemies only need to be outlived to be ultimately defeated.*

When this Tactical Objective is generated, nominate a **NECRONS CHARACTER** from your army. Score 1 victory point at the end of the game if this character is alive and on the battlefield.

## 15 — SLAUGHTER THE LIVING *Necrons*

*The young races cling to their primitive bodies of flesh and blood. Slaughter them like the animals they are, and reduce their corpses to their constituent atoms.*

Score 1 victory point if at least one enemy unit was completely destroyed during this turn.

## 13 — RECLAIM AND RECAPTURE *Necrons*

*Using hyperbinaric logic, key strategic targets have been identified. Your legions must reclaim them at all costs.*

Roll a D6 when this Tactical Objective is generated. If the result is an odd number, score D3 victory points if you control all 3 odd-numbered Objective Markers at the end of this turn. If the result is an even number, score D3 victory points if you control all 3 even-numbered Objective Markers at the end of this turn.

## 16 — CODE OF COMBAT *Necrons*

*Though the civilisations of today are little more than barbarians, the ancient codes of honourable combat must still be upheld.*

Score 1 victory point if a **NECRONS CHARACTER** killed an enemy **CHARACTER** during the Fight phase of this turn.

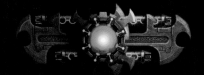